PERSPECTIVES ON MINORITY WOMEN
IN HIGHER EDUCATION

PERSPECTIVES ON MINORITY WOMEN IN HIGHER EDUCATION

Edited by
Lynne Brodie Welch

New York
Westport, Connecticut
London

Library of Congress Cataloging-in-Publication Data

Perspectives on minority women in higher education / edited by Lynne
Brodie Welch.
   p. cm.
   Includes bibliographical references and index.
   ISBN 0–275–93742–9
   1. Minority college students—United States.   2. Afro-American
college students.   3. Women college students—United States.
I. Welch, Lynne B.
LC3731.P48   1992
378.1'9829—dc20   91–28833

British Library Cataloging in Publication Data is available.

Library of Congress Catalog Card Number: 91–28833
ISBN: 0–275–93742–9

First published in 1992

Praeger Publishers, One Madison Avenue, New York, NY 10010
An imprint of Greenwood Publishing Group, Inc.

Printed in the United States of America

The paper used in this book complies with the
Permanent Paper Standard issued by the National
Information Standards Organization (Z39.48–1984).

10 9 8 7 6 5 4 3 2 1

Contents

Acknowledgments

I want to acknowledge the assistance of Drs. Rita Landino and Margaret Merrion in reviewing the individual chapters in this book for their presentation at the First, Second, and Third International Conferences for Women in Higher Education sponsored by the Univeristy of Texas at El Paso. My deepest appreciation is given to Rachel Veach for assistance in preparing this manuscript.

Introduction: Higher Education—A View from Minority Women

Lynne Brodie Welch

This book, *Perspectives on Minority Women in Higher Education*, was a direct result of the International Conferences for Women in Higher Education sponsored by the University of Texas at El Paso. As I listened to women who are ethnic minorities in the United States, I was struck by the commonalities in their themes. Clearly, they said, there was little in the literature that discussed minority women in higher education. In the following chapters, the authors will give insight into some of the roles, issues, and dilemmas of minority women in higher education. It is hoped that these commentaries and research results will increase understanding and stimulate further inquiry regarding women who are ethnic minorities in institutions of higher education.

The authors repeatedly remark that few ethnic minority women can be found in higher education. They suggest that the campus climates are not friendly to them. Several mention that because they are both female and a member of an ethnic minority group, they have two strikes against them. Subtle and not-so-subtle discrimination against ethnic minority women is identified. Some of the authors suggest remedies to this discrimination by confronting it and educating others regarding nondiscriminatory modes of functioning.

An issue of concern to many of the authors in this book was the need for sensitization to cultural differences. Not only is there a lack of understanding of cultural differences between ethnic groups, but as one author points out, there is a lack of understanding between intraethnic groups. Several authors suggest that a clear understanding of culturally determined behaviors such as personal space and communication patterns would assist in the retention of ethnic minority women on college campuses. These insights would help to break down some of the myths associated with particular ethnic minority groups.

The need for networking and support of minority women in higher education was identified by several of the authors. They found that a networking for minority women did not exist. Some of the authors suggest ways in which support systems can be developed. Mentoring by other women, whether or not they are a minority, was identified as a way to encourage the minority female to stay in and climb up the system in higher education.

The issue of being on the sidelines and not really being a "player" or being identified as a marginal person is discussed by several of the authors. In their view marginal individuals are simply not seen; they are ignored as if they don't even exist. Developing clear goals for oneself, learning how to negotiate the system, and finding a mentor are strategies that can assist the minority female in becoming a part of the system.

Roles that minority women themselves can take to mentor and network, both in the university environment and in communities, are identified. Of particular interest to me is the social responsibility that women in higher education have to their sisters. This social responsibility is to assist them in accessing education and higher education as well as impacting their own social and political environments. It is the hope of the authors that the issues discussed in the following chapters will begin to create understanding and dialogue about women who are an ethnic minority in higher education.

I

The Climate and Support Needs of Minority Women

In this section three authors identify some of the broader issues for minority women who function in the higher education environment. Denise Wilbur emphasizes the importance of each campus assessing the climate for women who are ethnic minorities. Her experience in developing a survey is highlighted. Strategies for asking the "right" questions are suggested. She stresses the importance of a welcoming campus atmosphere so that minority women can be recruited to and retained on a college campus.

Barbara Mathews stresses the importance of a campus community developing networking and support for women of color. Her experience in developing such supports is discussed. In her discussion of minority women dealing with The White Male System, Patricia Bassett emphasizes the need to understand The System in order to be able to function effectively. Bassett believes that minority women can be successful but that they must take responsibility for developing a plan for their career.

1

Conducting a Campus Climate Study for Women and Minorities

Denise Wilbur

Increasingly, on many campuses the retention of women and minorities as students, staff, and faculty is receiving as much emphasis as their recruitment. There is growing awareness that a hospitable and nourishing campus climate is necessary to guarantee diversity in higher education institutions. Women and people of color need to work in an environment that promotes their professional growth and development. There is growing recognition of the significant role campus climate plays in the retention of faculty, staff, and students. In an era that emphasizes commitment to diversity, it is important to ensure commitment to an equitable and hospitable climate for all members of a campus community. But how do institutions that, for the most part, continue to be managed and governed by white males determine if they have what is perceived as a welcoming environment?

In order to assess the campus climate, some institutions have begun to study their own environment. A comprehensive institutional assessment can explore the perceptions of the campus community and provide important information to inform future policy decisions—and, in some cases, to rectify past inequities.

In 1988, at the suggestion of the Student Affairs Committee of the Board of Trustees, the President of the College of St. Thomas requested that the Vice President for Student Affairs examine the campus climate for women and minorities. To facilitate this effort, the Vice President for Student Affairs convened a Campus Climate Task Force representing the various constituencies at the college: faculty, staff, and students. The project provided the committee members a unique opportunity for collaboration.

The committee designed the project in four phases: (1) survey design and development, (2) data collection and analyses, (3) task force discussion and recommendations, and (4) dissemination/reporting. The primary data came from a survey of faculty, staff, and students. In addition, focus groups were conducted to provide greater depth for the survey data.

During the fall 1988 semester, two methods of data collection were designed: survey instruments and focus groups. Early in 1989 surveys were distributed and focus groups were held. Three survey instruments were constructed and distributed to three groups on campus: students, faculty, and staff. The last group included administrative/professional staff as well as all positions of support staff. Recipients of the survey included men and women of all racial and ethnic backgrounds represented at the college.

The College of St. Thomas is one of the first of a growing number of higher education institutions to study the climate for women and one of a few to enlarge the project to include an examination of the climate for people of color. Also, the College of St. Thomas study is unique in other ways. Both men and women from all segments of the campus community participated in the study. The intent of the study was (1) to provide information to the President and Board of Trustees regarding the campus climate, (2) to assist the administration in an examination of policies that influence climate, (3) to provide faculty, staff, and students the opportunity to share their perceptions of the climate, and (4) to raise the awareness of the College of St. Thomas community to important climate issues.

Early in 1989 surveys were distributed and focus groups were held. Recipients included all the men and women who were employed as faculty and staff at the College of St. Thomas during Spring semester 1989. Surveys were mailed to a random sample of St. Thomas undergraduate and graduate students. Approximately two weeks after the initial mailing, a follow-up reminder was sent to all participants. This process yielded an overall response rate of 49%. Data were collected and tabulated throughout the spring of 1989.

In order to gather qualitative data on the perceived climate for women and minorities on campus, a series of focus groups involving faculty, staff, and students was scheduled in March 1989. The use of focus groups allowed for exploration of areas and ideas not easily accessible through use of a survey instrument. The focus group sessions provided the researchers with supplemental information to the survey and pertinent quotations.

SURVEY DESIGN

Although it is difficult to design a questionnaire that is relatively free of biases, the use of similar questions across populations helped to hold the bias constant across all respondents. The surveys also were examined for bias by two outside consultants. In order to increase the validity of the questionnaires, the members of the Campus Climate Task Force (representing a cross section of the campus population) reviewed each survey question for appropriateness of vocabulary, issue, and so forth. A pilot study of the three surveys was completed prior to the full-scale distribution of the instruments. Those completing the pilot questionnaires were interviewed to determine where they may have encountered difficulties with vocabulary or ambiguity. The questions were then modified where appropriate.

Anonymity and confidentiality were guaranteed to the survey respondents. There was no coding of the survey mailing—a procedure that facilitates follow-up mailings. Survey recipients were requested to return their surveys to the Office of Institutional Research (IR) in an enclosed, plain white, pre-addressed envelope. To further protect confidentiality all data entry was done by IR staff, thus limiting the number of people seeing the completed surveys.

The work of the Campus Climate Task Force was informed by a number of studies and publications. A natural starting point for a study of campus climate for women are three publications of the Project on the Status and Education of Women of the Association of American Colleges (AAC). Often referred to as the "chilly papers," the studies coauthored by Bernice Sandler and Rob Hall are *The Classroom Climate: A Chilly One for Women?* (1982); *Out of the Classroom: A Chilly Campus Climate for Women?* (1984); and *The Campus Climate Revisited: Chilly for Women Faculty, Administrators, and Graduate Students* (1986). The task force also examined other surveys. Most helpful was the *Gender Communication Questionnaire* designed by Alice Thomas, Director of the Office of Educational Research at St. Olaf College in Northfield, Minnesota. Also helpful were surveys used by the Great Lakes Colleges Association (GLCA) of Ann Arbor, Michigan, a consortium of twelve private liberal arts colleges in Indiana, Michigan, and Ohio. GLCA conducted studies on the quality of life for women students on the college campus, equity for women faculty, and a survey of female faculty experiences.

The College of St. Thomas surveys designed for students and faculty contained questions on classroom interactions and asked the respondents to identify the differences in behavior, if any, they had observed between female and male students as well as between majority and minority students. These included the following: interrupting another student before response is complete; attempting to intimidate the instructor; asking more questions in class; and assuming the role of leader when working in a mixed group. The student survey included questions on how often their courses included content on women and people of color. A section in the student survey on harassment included the following questions: Have you been addressed or referred to in sexual terms that made you feel uncomfortable by a faculty member, student, or staff member? Have you been touched in a way that made you feel uncomfortable by a faculty member, student, or staff member?

Surveys designed for faculty and staff included questions on collegial relations and college policies. Respondents were asked to rate their satisfaction with college efforts in a number of areas including hiring women and people of color as faculty and administrators and creating an equitable professional climate for women and people of color. Other questions included the following: Does your department demonstrate awareness of gender or minority concerns by discussing issues of curriculum, faculty/staff recruitment, and student recruitment at department meetings? How do you feel about the present composition of the top administration? All three surveys asked the respondents if they had ever felt unwelcome or intimidated anywhere on campus because of their gender or ethnicity.

Faculty surveys were sent to all the men and women who were teaching at the college during Spring semester 1989. This included adjunct and part-time faculty. The overall response rate was 54%; 79% of the women and 46% of the men responded.

Surveys were mailed to all staff members employed at all levels of the college. The overall response rate was 60%: 55% male and 64% female.

Surveys were mailed to a random sample of 700 undergraduate students and 500 graduate students. The random sample did not stratify the students by level, sex, major, or race. The overall student response rate was 43%.

FOCUS GROUPS

A series of focus groups were scheduled in order to gather qualitative data on the perceived climate for women and minorities on campus. The use of focus groups allowed for exploration of ideas and areas not easily accessible through use of survey instruments.

The focus groups involved faculty, staff, and students. Seventeen sessions were scheduled, most of them during campus-wide free periods or the lunch hour. Drawn from a random sample, 300 faculty and staff members received invitations to participate in a focus session. The invitations explained the nature and purpose of the study. An equal number of invitations were extended to men and women. The groups were sex segregated to allow greater freedom of expression and comfort for the participants. Each session was conducted by a member of the Campus Climate Task Force, and in a few of the sessions assistant moderators were present. Each session lasted about an hour.

Questions used in the focus groups were developed and reviewed by members of the Campus Climate Task Force. A pilot session was conducted with staff and faculty members who had expressed an interest in the work of the task force. Each group was asked the same list of core questions. A general question about the campus climate was used to begin each session and allow the participants an opportunity to speak and adjust to the group and the setting. Additional questions were asked as necessary to expand on an issue or to probe further into an area being discussed. Confidentiality was promised to group participants.

CONCLUSION

As a first step in an institutional assessment, the campus climate study provided data to support widely held opinions about the current climate on campus for women and people of color. The study examined perceptions on issues such as salary equity, hiring procedures, opportunity for advancement, and professional development. It provided a basis for further studies and an examination of policies. The report was discussed at an open forum on campus and is viewed as the starting point for further discussions. The report will also be used to inform the work of the Minority Task Force and the Affirmative Action Committee. An outgrowth of the study is the recent formation of a Gender Issues Task Force to continue the work begun by the climate study.

The project collected perceptions and experiences of both males and females; comparable information was gathered from all segments of the campus. Through the use of survey instruments and focus groups, both qualitative and quantitative data were generated.

By opting to develop our own instruments and conduct the research internally, the task force was able to shape a project suited to our needs and appropriate to our campus at a relatively low cost. The use of a sixteen-member task force prevented criticism of the study's findings and conclusions from being directed at one person or one department. The members of the task force also learned during the process of generating and evaluating the survey questions. Many lively discussions ensued. One especially lively discussion centered on what is meant by an "old boys' network" and whether it was appropriate to include a question about its existence on campus in the survey. It was included, and some of the men on the task force expressed surprise at the determination of the women on the task force to include it. By involving the entire campus community, at the very least, awareness of the issues was raised. Having both men and women respond to the survey and participate in focus groups provided interesting differences in perceptions of climate issues by gender. The small number of people of color on our campus meant that the information the study was able to gather was limited, but interesting observations about classroom interactions have provided the impetus for diversity workshops and seminars.

By designing and using information-gathering techniques unique to our institution, we generated important information. More important, these first assessment tools provided a basis for an ongoing dialogue as well as future programs that continue to emphasize a commitment to diversity and all that implies.

2

Networking and Support for Women of Color

Barbara Matthews

One of the issues for women in higher education, particularly for minority women, is the need for a campus climate that supports and nurtures them. Establishment of adequate support networks is one way in which to develop a campus that is friendly toward minority women. College campuses can be confusing and overwhelming to individuals who are new to the system. P. Rosa and E. Smith, in their report "Equity and Pluralism: Full Participation of Blacks and Hispanics in New England Higher Education" (1989), found that women and minority students often feel intimidated in such a setting. Finding 5A of their report stated that:

Blacks and Hispanics (and other populations) require a nurturing campus climate in order to succeed. Special encouragement was recommended by this Task Force in order to ensure that students receive the nurturing that is necessary for intellectual and personal growth, and essential for coping with a majority-determined educational setting.

According to C. Hetherinton and R. Barcelo (1985), women need to support and assist each other consciously. In their study "Womentoring: A Cross-Cultural Perspective," they observed that women empower other women to gain expertise and knowledge in their own right:

Cross-cultural womentoring builds effective work teams and enhances cross-cultural understanding and appreciation by building on the strengths within her own cultural framework, as opposed to attempting to shape Women of Color into their own image and values.

In his study of the "Family State College," W. Tierney (1988) explored the essential elements of organizational culture and found what he described as a "sense of family." According to Tierney, even in times of increasing complexity, a central goal of understanding organizational culture is necessary to minimize the occurrence and consequences of cultural conflict and to help foster the development of shared goals. The challenge is to identify those factors in a particular campus and to develop strategies to deal with them so that students become one of the family.

Women of Color have benefited from the expanded support of many vital groups who have assisted in the development and empowerment of women students and faculty of color. Her campus, located in a large urban community, has a student body of over 12,000, five percent of whom are Women of Color. The faculty and administrative staff also has approximately five percent Women of Color in its ranks. As a minority group, Women of Color often found that their minority voice and needs were ignored and many times unmet. In an effort to become an integral part of the university culture, Women of Color needed the support, encouragement, and inspiration of diverse groups within the university.

I myself have been intimately involved in the establishment of a network of groups who were vital to the support of Women of Color on the campus at Southern Connecticut State University. The network includes such diverse groups as the Black Student Union, the Organization of Latin American Students, the Black-Hispanic Consortium, the Women's Commission, the Women's Association, the People-to-People Club, and the Minority Women's Support Group. Each of these groups played a unique part in the development of a campus climate that is friendly toward minority women.

The Black Student Union is an activity-based group that sponsors cultural programs and current events seminars of particular interest to Black students. This group sponsored several seminars that were of particular interest to Women of Color. In addition to stimulating interest in and discussion of the topic, they provided a mechanism for networking, sharing, and mutual support.

As a broadly based group of faculty, students, and administrators, the Black-Hispanic Consortium assists students to identify and achieve goals related to employment. It also sponsors educational activities that assist members toward achieving their employment goals. The Consortium was particularly helpful in assisting Women of Color to identify their strengths and develop career and employment goals that reflected a particular individual's strengths and abilities. The People-to-People Club linked foreign students and faculty with American faculty and students. Many of the Women of Color on campus participated in the cross-cultural experiences and activities sponsored by this group.

The Women's Commission, consisting of women students, faculty, administrators, and staff, developed policies and programs that directly affected all women at the university. Particularly useful to Women of Color on campus was the establishment of day care, a Women's Center, and a rape crisis network system. In addition, the linkage and coordination function of this group enabled Women of Color to have access to information and decision making at all levels of the university. The Women's Association, consisting of female faculty and faculty wives, funded scholarships for Women of Color and served as an emergency loan resource for students. More than once these loans enabled a Woman of Color to continue her education at the university.

Of particular importance to Women of Color was the Minority Women's Support Group, which was sponsored by the Office of Minority Affairs. This sister-to-sister support group met regularly to share concerns and offer support to the minority women who attended. Bonding and confidentiality permitted the women to experience a significant dimension of personal awareness. It enabled them to learn about the culture of the university, develop a sense of family, and experience acceptance into the campus environment.

As the entire university community has become more aware of the rewards of cultural diversity, I find that cross-cultural exchange is flourishing on my campus. Specifically, in many women's groups the majority of women who are in positional power are assisting minority women to move into the mainstream. As each campus group seeks to accomplish its individual objectives through sponsored activities, they have been openly receptive to the goals of the Women of Color on campus. By increasing their interaction these groups have encouraged and empowered Women of Color to excel and succeed in a friendly environment. The goals of sharing and networking have brought greater vitality to all of the groups. In the process, the overall organizational culture has been moved into a greater sense of family, "Southern style."

3

Resolving Pink and Brown Conflicts Resulting from the White Male System

Patricia Bassett

As the higher education work force becomes diversified, a number of difficulties arise because women of color pursue limited opportunities in institutions dominated by white males. Yet there is an increasing tendency to deny the great impact of race on higher education administration. White males in particular do not like to think of themselves as unfair, because they have ideals of equality, freedom, and so forth. Furthermore, it is difficult for white males to recognize that women, especially minority women, face a more hostile atmosphere and double discrimination because they are competing with white males for limited lucrative middle- and upper-level management positions.

In order to survive conflicts resulting from limited and controlled opportunities, one must closely examine the dynamics that disable women, especially women of color. One of the critical elements is understanding the white male agenda and the resulting stereotypes that adversely impact women and people from various racial groups. The impact of the White Male System is so subtly intertwined in academe that it is difficult to discern. It is important that all women understand how the male system causes conflicts and has an adverse effect on male relationships with women as they pursue positions of authority. H. Austin and A. Bayer (1972) state that the academic reward system is biased toward behaviors and activities exhibited primarily by men. Furthermore, since men established the system, rewards go primarily to women who accept and share male criteria for academic success. A conscious decision must be made to decipher the interactive white male system and plan strategies to neutralize its devastating impact on women. Understanding the negative impact of the White Male System will enable women to develop and practice behaviors that empower each other rather than promote or reinforce male oppression.

DEFINING THE WHITE MALE SYSTEM

In my opinion, A. Schaef (1985) best describes the myths that underline components of a White Male System. It is important to understand this system because the roots of sexism and racism derive from it. The first tenet of the White Male System is the belief that the male system is the only one that exists and that, therefore, the male system is the right and only way of life. All other perceptions are viewed as incorrect, stupid, invalid, incompetent, or crazy. Accordingly, men in the male-dominated institutions tend to discount, disparage, destroy, or minimize other perceptions. The system consistently and methodically denies or questions the perceptions and experiences of women and minority groups.

Another myth of the White Male System is that white men have the birthright to be innately superior. Anyone who does not belong to this system is innately inferior. Hence, it is difficult for males in this system to admit mistakes or judgement errors. Severe problems exist because individuals believe they possess power and influence just by being born male or white. A man can be less competent than a woman, but he still has the advantage over her because he is a man. Unfortunately, women and minority groups are unaware that they reinforce the myth that white men understand and know everything. Thus, they contribute to and sustain the white male illusion by frequently looking to white males for advice and direction. Consciously or unintentionally, white women join white males to sabotage the authority and career plans of women of color, giving them a competitive edge over women of color. White women have one strike against them—being female; women of color have two strikes against them—being female and racially different.

Another myth of the White Male System is that men are logical, rational, and totally objective, while women and minorities are illogical and out of control. Living with this myth can mean living in ignorance while overlooking the virtues and abilities of others. White males appear to have an overwhelming need to hold on to their sense of superiority. There is an innate fear that if others are equal then white males are somehow worthless. This is the main reason why many white males fear women and minorities who obtain positions of power. Recently, a white male colleague admitted to me, "If women and minorities take the power from us, you all will do the same thing to us as we've done to you." One can see why many white men exercise control to limit the number of women and minorities in positions of authority.

One does not have to be a white male to accept and support the White Male System. Unbeknown to many, women and people from various ethnic and racial groups may inadvertently support the White Male System. This point was best illustrated in the recent movie *Driving Miss Daisy*. One scene depicts a crowd of people watching a black man who is trapped on an elevator. The president of the company, a Jewish man, had called a repair man hours earlier. From the back of the crowd a black man with broken English gives instruction to the man trapped in the elevator and he is freed. The look of disgust and disapproval among the crowd is apparent because the black man knew something that the Jewish man did not know. In reality, almost all women and other minority groups feel trapped. It is easy to understand why women and minorities have learned that "we can't let them know that we know more. We'll lose our jobs if they find out that they aren't superior."

White females should avoid falling into the trap of attacking other women and minority females just so that they themselves will be one up on status with white males. These attacks on women, and minority women in particular, are ever so subtle. Yolanda Moses (1989) states in "Black Women in Academe" that both white males and females misinterpret the behavior of black women who lead. For example, a black woman's silence is interpreted as sullenness. On the other hand, assertive remarks made by black women are viewed as confrontive or disrespectful.

LIMITED RESOURCES AND AFFIRMATIVE ACTION

Over the years, position changes have become the primary means for advancing women and minorities into leadership positions and into administrative jobs (Sagaria 1988). Competition for good jobs in part intensifies the depth of the threat felt by white males. Once a minority is perceived as taking something to which the dominant group feels exclusively entitled, it becomes subjected to harassment, exploitation, manipulation, and oppression by the dominant group. Whites develop negative stereotypes to justify the exploitation of and discrimination against minorities. Negative stereotypes about African Americans are the most common and resilient. Fernandez (1981) found that more than half of all black managers (males, 55 percent; females, 49 percent) believe minorities are penalized more for mistakes than are whites. He concludes that "regardless of what has been said about the different experiences of minorities, the important point to remember is that the responses of white Americans to the competition of minorities typically has been to blame the victims of racism—the minorities—and not the perpetrators of racism—the whites themselves. Thus, racism became an ever-expanding vortex fueled by greed and fears on the part of whites and anger and paranoia on the part of minorities" (p. 24).

The minority group's behavior is largely reactive. Many whites view minority groups as a threat to the status quo. They fear the loss of power, control, and social position. This power struggle has caused competition for scarce resources such as jobs.

The White Male System gives males a false sense of superiority, resulting in gender and racial stereotypes that must be maintained to keep the dominant system intact. Schaef (1985) states that a stereotype is the definition of one group of persons by another group of persons who wishes to control the first group. In order to deal with women and minority groups, the dominant system neatly describes and categorizes members of groups that support the illusions and myths of the system. African Americans were the first group to defy the truism and stereotypes given them by the White Male System.

T. Ruble, R. Cohen, and D. Ruble (1984) state that occupational stereotypes and oversimplifications operate in various ways to limit employment opportunities. These biases are subtle and present an overabundance of hurdles that eliminate competent women. They limit career advancement of those women who survive the system. For instance, white males and some white females believe minority managers use race as an alibi for many difficulties they have on the job. Thus, many whites dismiss legitimate minority complaints simply because they come from minorities. Participants in the White Male System try to make the minority person feel guilty, that something is wrong with the minority person because she/he has problems. Other supervisors believe that minority women come from cultural backgrounds that are not conducive to successful management and therefore are not as qualified as most white administrators.

Many white administrators admit to having negative stereotypes about minorities but claim these attitudes do not affect their behavior toward them. Minority female administrators must interact effectively with whites every day in order to be successful in the male system. Few white administrators go that extra mile to effectively interact with minorities. White administrators feel uncomfortable dealing with minority women but do not identify or acknowledge their own uncertainties as the root of the problems. For example, minority women are excluded from informal work networks by white males. Furthermore, minority females are excluded from social activities and informal work networks that are beneficial to advancement in higher education. One African American woman stated, "My peers never invite me to informal discussions, meetings, and luncheons, and many times they discuss issues related to my job." The consequences of excluding and bypassing any administrator can be detrimental to organizational effectiveness and efficiency. White administrators may feel that minority managers got their jobs because of equal employment opportunity (EEO) targets and not because of their abilities.

THE CAREER TRAP

Minority women must be better performers than whites to get ahead. Yet many times minority women are placed in dead-end jobs. In addition, careers may be held up because departments are reluctant to give up the minority because of their departmental EEO goals.

Changing Rules, Double Standards

In visiting with other black women in higher education, I have learned that their experiences are similar to my own. It is difficult to keep up with the ever-changing procedures of an organization. Minority women learn the rules and attempt to follow them carefully in the hope of becoming like everyone else and blending in. But just as soon as you develop some expertise in the organization's rules, someone changes the rules. Then the system will punish you for not knowing that the rules changed, even though information was not given about the change. A perceptive individual can sometimes pick up cues by watching the white male behavior. I have noted that sometimes the men just stop following the rules. Perhaps white men believe that since they make the rules, they can also break them or change them at will. If clarification is sought, the response makes the questioner feel stupid for asking in the first place.

Promotions and Career Traps

W. Swuderski (1988) summarized three major concerns for women who become administrators: entry, survival, and advancement. Entry for women of color in higher education administration starts off at a disadvantage because many people believe women of color have decided advantages over others in the employment market. One of the disturbing aspects of this point of view is that special intelligence, abilities, and skills of individuals who just happen to be minority are not acknowledged. Women of color continue to face unique challenges. One of the major challenges is the inability of others to discern and/or separate race and gender issues. Daily decisions must be made by women of color to deny, ignore, or challenge racist or sexist issues.

Institutions that are serious about hiring and developing minority women need to evaluate these critical issues. Several creative strategies can be formulated that result in prolonged success and personal growth of capable women. For example, postsecondary executives must examine the biases and attitudes of the power base in the institution. In addition, administrators must recognize the various manifestations of jealous behaviors from constituents in the immediate and surrounding work environment of minority women.

To complicate matters many white, middle-aged, middle-level college degree managers feel frustrated with their jobs and the lack of advancement opportunities. One "seasoned" male colleague of mine said, "Today things are half backwards. Women supervise men, minorities get all the opportunities, and the younger, inexperienced administrators question the authority of seasoned ones." This gentleman further stated that hard work, ability, and merit are no longer of value, that minorities and women are promoted regardless of qualifications. White males, especially older ones, have no opportunities for advancement and believe that they are discriminated against.

Minority women feel that rewards for ability, merit, and hard work are a reality only for white men. In their opinion, minorities and women are excluded from informal work groups by whites. They are told directly and indirectly that they got their jobs because of quotas, not because of their abilities. They believe that white males have the power, that they promote white males 95 percent of the time, and that equal opportunity employment laws are easily circumvented. This means that women and minorities are not promoted and are put into stifling, dead-end jobs with little power.

The conflict between the needs and aspirations of the individuals and the goals and requirements of the organization has always been present. One of the forces changing the value system of the historically dominating white male is the combined effect of equal employment opportunity legislation and Affirmative Action programs (EEO/AAP). They have created a more heterogeneous work force. Although the work force is diverse it is by no means perfect. The diversity has caused conflict and stress. P. Bronstein, L. Black, J. Pfennig, and A. White (1986) discovered that while females were at least as well qualified as males, females tended to obtain jobs with lower status at institutions of lower prestige. The older the worker, the lower the manifest strength of the work ethic. One possible explanation for this is that younger workers tend to believe hard work and good performance lead to jobs that are interesting and challenging as well as to promotional opportunities and fair treatment. As the individual grows older she/he learns that hard work and good performance on the job do not necessarily lead to such rewards. Thus, they become less work oriented in later years as the institutional culture becomes more apparent.

Fernandez (1981) found that in the past, white men dominated 95 percent of management ranks while representing only 37 percent of the population. Today these white men must compete with women and minorities (63 percent of the population) with whom they have never had to compete. Thus, many of these white males truly believe that they are treated unfairly and that reverse discrimination is a common occurrence.

In contrast, large numbers of women and minorities believe that even after twenty years of equal employment opportunity, white men are still the favored group. This phenomenon of disparate perceptions contributes to the differences between people who have been accustomed to having almost all of the managerial power and people who have had almost none.

While many unanticipated conflicts occur overtly, there is also more subtle self-destructive displacement when conflict is ignored. In addition to decreasing the institution's potential for an open, creative, and friendly atmosphere, hidden conflict can be reflected in tardiness, absenteeism, high turnover, and production errors and grievances. Unresolved conflict may cause stress-related physical symptoms such as insomnia, headache, hypertension, cardiac irregularities, weight changes, ulcers, colitis, anxiety, depression, and burnout.

The Peter Principle states that in a hierarchy employees tend to rise to their level of incompetence. White men still have the major power to promote. Since most promotions are based on present performance, conformity, and likability by key people, rather than on the potential to perform the proposed job, many employees are promoted until they reach positions they can no longer handle in the most competent manner. To the institution's detriment, these employees are likely to stay in such positions. Even for white men the promotion system has never been strictly based on merit or ability. Those white men who fit rigid and subjective characteristics and attitudes of the vast majority are promoted to the upper levels of management. When social criteria serve as measurement surrogates, managers tend to reproduce themselves through promotion of those similar to themselves. Filling management slots with people similar to themselves reinforces the belief that such people deserve high-level positions. Managerial cloning serves as a risk reduction mechanism for the group in power.

Many policies are not uniform or well defined. Therefore, they can be subject to a high degree of subjectivity and political influence. Many white males believe that promotional policies strongly influenced by EEO/AAP provide preferential treatment to women and minorities.

When women and minorities ask questions about their job performance, potential evaluations, and career plans, older managers believe that these questions demonstrate aggressiveness and lack discretion.

While many minorities and women fight over only a small portion of the pie, white men sit back and continue to feast on the largest portion. While some legitimate reasons exist for white men who work at entry level jobs to feel that their opportunities have decreased, white men represent only 37 percent of the U.S. population and have totally dominated the managerial profession since its beginning. When laws were introduced forcing them to compete with the remaining 63 percent of the population, they began to recognize that their career opportunities and power would greatly be reduced if the laws were fully implemented. The increased competition does not apply to well-qualified, high-performing, high-potential white men but rather to the great masses of average and below-average white men who got their positions because of explicit or implicit preference based on race and gender. A white male colleague states that he believes "that EEO/AAP affects only the marginally qualified white male." In the view of black women, whites make the major decisions, many of which reflect racist and gender preferences and attitudes. The myth that minorities and women are making big gains at the expense of white males is allowed to persist. This belief in the myth in itself limits the number of minorities and women that get hired or promoted. One black female colleague states that "cries against preference were not voiced by white men when the quotas were 98 to 100 percent in their favor." It is easily understood that those in power would not relinquish any of that power voluntarily.

Support from Bosses

Women who believe in fairness may think that bosses want to assist their subordinates because of mutual dependency for success. When supervisors have negative feelings toward subordinates, they may deliberately withhold information or support in order to assert authority, increase dependency, or prove that the subordinate is not competent. The boss's evaluations may be influenced by subjective opinions or even unsubstantiated facts. Furthermore, the boss may not be sufficiently aware of the subordinate's contributions.

Some whites are unable to work comfortably with minority managers. Minority female administrators do not have the same power as whites in similar positions because their authority is constantly being undermined. For example, subordinates often bypass a minority female administrator and go directly to her superiors. Bypassing a person because she/he is a minority or woman not only undermines her/his authority and position but also smacks of racism and sexism. A supervisor's acceptance of deliberate disruption of the chain of command because of race or gender perpetuates stereotyped attitudes about women and minorities. It also gives the impression that the administrator who was bypassed does not have the ability to do the job. Fortunately, not all participate in this undermining, but respect is the exception rather than the rule.

In addition to lack of support, double standards are applied to both women and women of color. Men are expected to travel, give speeches, attend meetings, or consult with their colleagues at other institutions; such activities are assumed to be a part of their administrative duties. However, when the administrator is a woman, the men she supervises complain that she is never there. They unconsciously expect a woman administrator to be available.

Schaef (1985) says that most women use fairness as a strategy. She believes women are noted for fairness even if it is at their own expense. Most women and minorities believe justice and fairness exist in the legal system. We forget that laws are made by the White Male System to promulgate its values and support its myths. When many of us collide with the White Male System, we expect that the truth will bring forth justice. White males often change the rules midstream without informing others.

RECOMMENDATIONS

Interestingly enough, I have found that white females best understand the White Male System. Sensitive and fair white females can be especially skillful in helping white men understand the plight of black women who lead. Once the white female understands the White Male System, she can use that system for her own benefit or participate with a core of individuals who insist on fair and unbiased standards. She will remember that women of color face double discrimination and she will make a conscious effort not to support such discrimination.

In summary, minority women can become successful in white male systems through taking responsibility for initiating and communicating a plan for their own growth and development in predominantly white institutions. Minority women must recognize that their growth and pursuit of excellence pose threats to insecure colleagues and superiors. At some point minority women may have to learn how to manage superiors whose professional skills are not as good as their own. Ultimately, minority women must learn to evaluate which battles are worth fighting and which should be ignored. Meanwhile, minority women can help themselves by:

1. Working with key administrators to develop an employment atmosphere that has individuality, creativity, honesty, and an acceptance of diversity as its main tenets.

2. Helping men and white females recognize the destructive and costly results of racism and sexism in higher education.

3. Developing programs to educate administrators on racism and sexism and to help the administrator to explore how diversity enhances the academic environment.

4. Working with key university administrators to provide a strong EEO/AAP emphasis and programs that include specific immediate sanctions against those who violate its philosophies and tenets.

II

African American Women and Higher Education

In this section three authors look at African American women in higher education. Eleanor Smith and Paul Smith, Jr., discuss the long and rich legacy of African American women in the development of higher education in the United States. They emphasize the influence that early role models had in enabling African American women to be successful in the higher education environment.

Mary Ann Williams emphasizes the importance of communication for African American women in higher education. She suggests that cultural patterns of communication need to be understood by all concerned. M. Colleen Jones studies the black woman presidents of colleges and universities in the United States. She finds that there is little literature on black woman presidents and suggests that the personal and other factors that lead to their leadership development would have implications for the nurturing of other black women interested in leadership positions in higher education.

II

African American
Women and Higher
Education

4

The Legacy of African American Women in Higher Education

Eleanor J. Smith and Paul M. Smith, Jr.

Today there are many successful African American women in higher education administration. Most of these women are in responsible positions because of their various traits, skills, and desires to learn what the demands and opportunities of this society require. The physical and cultural uniqueness of their Africanness has attracted biases of the Western world. Their negative and positive experiences have combined to promote the development of their being as well as their careers. It is this mix of negative and positive experiences, weaknesses and strengths, that accounts for their ability to stay the course and conquer the challenges of administrative work. However, a deeper and more inspiring claim to their margins of success remains unstated by the historical world of their female ancestors. This chapter will attempt to indicate that closer relationship. The purpose of this inquiry is to (1) infer how select women from the ancient African past and during slavery used their leadership and management skills to motivate others to improve their chances in life, (2) examine the administrative skills of four women who created and directed educational institutions, and (3) suggest how these experiences can further reinforce the status of women in higher education administration today.

Perhaps most women obtained many of their management and organizational skills from the demands of informal activities that centered around home life. However, most of the women alluded to in this chapter have extended themselves far beyond the family circle. Their premier skills have been merged and developed from formal learning and extended experiences with people in industry, organizations, and institutions. Consequently, the term "leadership" is used to convey the notion of guiding to inspire and/or empower others. Administrative skills are used to extend the meaning and values in an institutional and organized effort.

HERITAGE

Although many African American women may not be able to make a direct connection between themselves and thousands of years of ancestral contributions, there is no doubt that African and African American women had their origin on the continent of Africa. Humankind evolved from the Pygmy people located in the lake region of central Africa, the source of the Nile. In the beginning, humans expressed themselves with few words but with many signs, symbols, or sign language (Churchward 1978). As civilization moved up the Nile Valley, it was the Egyptians who preserved much of this ancient information. It was derived from decoding the hieroglyphics found in the Pyramid texts of Pepi I and II and the Coffin text of Amamu. Women were involved with organizing the innermost concerns of humankind's destiny. In the Legend of Osiris, who died and returned to eternal life, it was Isis who searched and found the body parts of her husband Osiris so that life could be sustained. From this effort she helped spread the ideas of life, suffering, death, resurrection, eternal life, and supporting rituals (Budge 1967). Woman was thought to be symbolic of life. She was viewed as representative of a goddess who was made fertile from the rain and sun in the sky, and from the earth that nurtured the seed of vegetation resembling her bosom, which gave birth to life. From the observations of sky, earth, and vegetation the triad of demi-gods evolved into Isis, Osiris, and Horus. Isis and the baby Horus represented the Virgin birth, thus the Black Madonna became a symbol around which religion organized worship. This experience has become part of the basic belief system found in many religious practices throughout the Christian world (Diop 1959).

In Africa the first organized human group was matriarchal. Everyone was considered a descendant of the mother, in that the identification of the father was known only to her (Jackson 1970). Furthermore, woman was pivotal to the organization of the family for survival. In the early human economy the first tools were made for women; they gathered four-fifths of the food supply, including plants, eggs, ants, and honey.

Men hunted meat, providing one-fifth of the food supply. The sharing of the two operations fostered cooperation for a developing human existence (Leakey 1978).

African American women may be inspired by the leadership qualities of Queen Hatshepsut, who ruled Egypt 1,500 years before the birth of Christ and who organized the first trade expedition to the land of Punt. In 960 B.C. Queen Makeda (Queen of Sheba) ruled Ethiopia and planned an arduous journey to Jerusalem to learn the wisdom of King Solomon. She built the capital city, naming it Debra Makeda after herself. In 69 B.C. Cleopatra and her brother, Ptolemy XIII, ruled Egypt together during troubled times. Queen Nzingha of Ndongo/Kongo successfully resisted the Portuguese occupation with a fierce army of women warriors from 1623 to 1663. She also organized the Moni-Kongo groups, national and international, to oppose European domination of Africa (Williams 1974). Other African women who organized resistance to the slave trade and the colonial system were Madame Tinubu of Nigeria; Nandi, mother of Chaka, the Zulu warrior; the female army led by the Dahomian King Bowelle; and the brave Yaa Asantewa, Queen Mother of the Ashanti people of Ghana, who led the war against the British in 1805. The Yaa Asantewa War was the last major one led by a woman in Africa (Diop 1959). This historical message demonstrates that women provided leadership and managed the affairs of states and institutions. Although some African women were forced to leave their country, they did not forget all of their cultural knowledge. It was this social, political, and economic foundation upon which they structured their understanding for a new beginning under different circumstances in a new land.

SELF AND SLAVERY

When a woman is taken from her home base by force, the only saving grace is a sense of self. Unless there is a balance between the psychological and physical to save the self for another day of life, death can seem the only solution. This was the answer for some, but for most African women the choice was to undergo the pain of slavery with all its unknowns and problems so that a generation of others could fight for a better existence. During this time leadership and direction were used individually and collectively to adjust to and help define a different cultural existence that would become more humane to African people. Perhaps the most difficult aspect of slave life was the daily disrespect and abuse from most white people. The basis for this mistreatment was skin color bias reinforced by laws that denied equal protection, rights, and freedom of choice. Thus, African American women recognized the necessity to prepare themselves and their families to read and write. Words on paper were a determinant to their development whether they

involved the Black Codes, the "three-fifths of a man" clause in the
Constitution, or laws such as those passed in South Carolina in 1740
that prohibited slaves from being taught to read and write (McKissick
1969).

Freedom of mind and body was paramount to African American wom-
en's existence, learning, development, and full participation in the society. One of the most daring leadership acts and messages relative to
the freedom goals was made by Harriet Tubman, who was born a slave
in 1823. Not only did she escape from a Maryland plantation to Phila-
delphia, but in spite of the $40,000 bounty issued for her head, she
returned to the South several times to help her family and some three
hundred slaves escape to the North via the Underground Railroad. This
was a signal of hope because the majority of African women were se-
verely exploited as child bearers and home and field workers for three
centuries without pay. Many others were convinced to exist as concu-
bines and were given empty promises. Yet in spite of such difficulties
many women were able to assert themselves toward the goal of education with the help of interested whites and freemen who were more
concerned with their advancement.

This commitment to self-development regardless of the odds against
success helped them reach their goals for education. There were clan-
destine schools in the woods and slave quarters at night. Milla Grenson
taught midnight school in Natchez, Louisiana (Lerner 1973). Freedmen
petitioned the state of Massachusetts for the right to attend the free
schools of Boston in 1787 (Aptheker 1973). Volunteers such as Margaret
Douglass were found guilty of teaching Sunday School to slaves (Lerner
1972). The National Female Anti-Slavery Society denounced racial prejudice and supported racial integration of churches and schools. Aboli-
tionist Prudence Crandall of Connecticut was taken to court because she
integrated her school. This school was denied existence by the state
court system and when that did not stop the activities, it was finally
closed because of a fire bombing (Aptheker 1982). The determination to
teach the rudiments of education involved the Freedman's Bureau,
which was organized in 1865 by the federal government to educate freed
women after the Civil War. Federal troops were used to provide some
protection against organized Southern whites' hostility, since there were
many who did not want freed women to become educated during the
Reconstruction Period (Davis 1981).

Now that the fight for education was viewed as a means of uplifting
African American women, all kinds of new developments took place.
In 1793 Catherine Ferguson, a teacher, opened a school for forty-eight
poor children in New York City. At the age of fifteen Ann Marie Becraft
founded in 1805 the first seminary boarding school for girls of African
descent in Washington, D.C. (Davis 1981). Mary Smith Peake organized

a school for fugitive slaves in her home in 1847. At about this time in Hampton, Virginia, Janie Porter Barrett opened the Palace-of-Delight in her home for the children and adolescents of the community. Carrie A. Tuggle opened the Tuggle Institute in 1903 for orphans in Birmingham, Alabama (Davis 1981). These are a very few of the women administrators to whom we owe a debt of gratitude for giving meaning and direction in education when times were tough and dangerous.

Whether they worked in houses, barns, churches, or in the woods, these women were pioneers in founding institutions. These early educators not only had to have the ability to direct the affairs of the school, but they had to have teaching skills to effectively reach the uniqueness of individual students. In almost all cases they had to act as a parent to explain morals, manners, and everyday health habits. This was necessary because the everyday pressures of making a living did not allow the parents time or knowledge for preparing their offspring for life in a capitalist society. These women had to improvise, organize make-do solutions, maintain expectations that would encourage positive development for most of their students, and use their common sense psychology to deal with parents and the public.

These efforts to promote education were furthered with the passage of certain amendments to the Constitution: the Thirteenth Amendment, abolishing slavery in 1865; the Fourteenth, granting citizenship, due process, and equal protection of the law in 1868; and the Fifteenth, granting voting rights in 1869. African American women had to be concerned with the dominance of males in the business of education. Although the Morrill Acts of 1863 and 1890 were responsible for founding several state land-grant colleges for African Americans in the South and West, the majority of trustees, presidents, and faculties were white males. This situation has not changed significantly except that now the administrators of these institutions are African American males (Barry and Blassingame 1982). Today, no more than four women serve as presidents of colleges where the student enrollment is chiefly African American. There are more than one hundred such institutions. In view of these challenges, African American women have continued to learn and show their skills where opportunities have arisen. For some, the pride they feel in their achievements stands as evidence and support from the distant sisterhood of those nineteenth-century administrators who led the way with ideas, persistence, and scarce financial resources.

LEADERSHIP

To illustrate further the paths taken and the leadership skills developed by selected African American women, we have chosen to review the work of Lucy Craft Laney, Nannie Helen Burroughs, Mary McLeod

Bethune, and Charlotte Hawkins Brown. These women were willing to sacrifice and follow their plan to build institutions where young women and men could prepare themselves for life in the United States. With little more than courage they were unafraid to take a risk to invest their time, energy, and resources in people and property. Each of these leaders had qualities that enabled them to get along with people who agreed, and in some instances disagreed, with their goals and directions. As effective educational administrators they proceeded with creations of their own or revised ideas to make their undertaking suitable to conditions for their purpose. Each gave of themselves by emulating a sense of values, goals, direction, and meaning that contributed to the education of young African Americans. Their effectiveness as administrators is evident by some of the many successful activities they initiated.

Lucy Craft Laney

"The educated Negro woman, the woman of character and culture is needed in the schoolroom. . . . only those of character and culture can do successful lifting for she who would mould character must herself possess it" (Lowenburg and Bogin 1976, p. 296). These are the words that helped set the sight of Lucy Craft Laney, who built and directed the Haines Normal and Industrial Institute in Augusta, Georgia. Lucy was born in 1854 of free and literate parents. Her childhood days were spent in the family home of working parents. She learned to read and write with the assistance of the people who employed her mother. All of the library sources of their home were open for her use. She was well prepared for a successful experience in high school and was a member of the first graduating class of Atlanta University in 1873. She taught for ten years in the public schools, and for a brief period she served as principal of a school in Savannah. Her keen sense of commitment to the cause of African American women was aroused by an article in the *Savannah Daily News* that threatened their livelihood, accusing them of being poor providers of care for white children. Lucy resolved to educate African American girls to become teachers capable of uplifting through convincing actions and of reaching out to serve their people as well as humankind (Daniel 1970).

Lucy Laney began this program of work by opening a school with six students in the basement of a church. This start was extended to a day and boarding school with only the blessing of the Presbyterian Board of Mission for Freedmen. Lack of money was a constant problem, motivating Lucy Laney to appeal to the General Assembly of the Presbyterian Church. With the assistance and encouragement of F. E. Haines, secretary of the Women's Executive Committee and the woman for whom the school was named, Lucy gained an immediate $10,000, many friends among the board members, and more contributors to the finances of the Institute. It was this use of good human relations and management that convinced a friend and donor to save the school from closing when the dormitory was destroyed by fire. In two years the enrollment increased to 234, and by 1940 1,000 students were enrolled. Lucy Laney also developed the first kindergarten in Augusta and opened a program for the education of nurses. Accomplishing such goals required that she spend all her personal savings and borrow funds so that young women and men could prepare themselves for work in the world community. She knew that the future of her students required a broad education. In spite of the argument suggesting that the educational experience of African Americans be limited to industrial education, Ms. Laney taught her students Latin, the classics, and algebra (Daniel 1970). As a result of this preparation, many of her students became outstanding citizens. John Hope became the President of Atlanta University. Many became commissioned officers in the armed forces, and Fannin Belcher, one of the first six students, had a successful practice as a physician in Savannah, Georgia. Many of Laney's students followed in her footsteps and became teachers. Mary McLeod Bethune chose Haines Normal and Industrial Institute to gain some of her early teaching experience (Daniel 1970).

Lucy C. Laney was a successful administrator because she was not too proud to ask for help. She demonstrated self-confidence, competence, and good human relations and management skills that were agreeable with supporters, and she was willing to make sacrifices. She paid her dues to the public by working with the Red Cross, Salvation Army, and Interracial Committees. Lucy Laney was recognized for her work in education by Lincoln, Atlanta, and Howard Universities, each of which awarded her an honorary master of arts degree.

Charlotte Hawkins

The leadership and administrative qualities of Charlotte Hawkins became evident because of the deep emotional drive of her inner qualities, as well as her ability and urge to achieve. She was born in 1882 in Henderson, North Carolina. Her mother took her to Cambridge, Massachusetts, where she was reared and educated in a comfortable home with her stepfather. Charlotte was not encouraged to attend college because her mother thought high school was enough schooling. Nevertheless, Charlotte wanted to attend college but had no means of financial support until Alice Freeman Palmer, a member of the State Board of Education of Massachusetts, spoke with her by chance on the street. Subsequently Palmer agreed to pay all her expenses to the State Normal school. Charlotte took advantage of this opportunity and attended Salem

State Teachers College and later took courses at Harvard and Simmons Colleges.

In Sedalia, North Carolina, where Palmer Memorial Institute was founded, Charlotte obtained her first teaching position at an American Missionary Association supported school. It paid $30 a month. In 1902, at the age of twenty, she opened a school with the money received from singing and speaking at summer resort hotels. With a sizeable donation from the Rosenwald Fund and contributions from northern and southern whites, Palmer was built as a finishing school for girls. Boys were later permitted to enroll in the million-dollar-plus plant of 350 acres (Giddings 1984). Although she married Edward S. Brown at age twenty-nine, this did not prevent Charlotte from continuing to meet the educational and cultural needs of the community.

Parents who sent their children to Palmer Memorial Institute called it either Palmer or the school run by Charlotte Hawkins Brown. The educational experiences were organized to prepare youth for college. The majority of her students were influenced in this direction, in that they came from middle-class families. Palmer was known for strict discipline, neat dress, good manners, and a liberal arts curriculum with emphasis on the theater, arts, and cultural subjects. Most graduates were likely to succeed in college.

The type of school Charlotte Hawkins Brown was trying to maintain required a great deal of capital for day-to-day operations. Her financial needs were complicated by unexpected tragedies such as the fires that destroyed the industrial building in December 1917 and the largest dormitory the following year (Daniel 1970). She realized the need to prepare a financial foundation for the school in the event she was no longer present. Toward this end she proposed raising $500,000 to begin an endowment (Lerner 1973). She persuaded the Board of Trustees to affiliate with the American Missionary Association to provide a source of steady financial support. The agreement for such support would become operational providing that $30,000 a year be raised for five years. She wrote hundreds of letters by hand in which she urged, begged, and pleaded for funds (Lerner 1973). Doctor Brown, as she was often called, raised more than $310,000 (Daniel 1970). Because she was dynamic, a good speaker, and a very effective manager of everyday matters, fundraising was a success at Palmer while she lived.

Palmer Memorial Institute owed its existence to the tremendous popularity, resilience, and strength of President Charlotte Hawkins Brown. She also served as President of North Carolina Negro State Teachers Association, North Carolina Federation of Women's Clubs, and Vice President of the National Association of Colored Women. She was a governor-appointed member of the North Carolina Council of Defense, a council member of the YWCA National Board for Interracial Cooperation, and she took part in the International Congress of Women. She passed away in 1961.

Nannie Helen Burroughs

In 1907, while serving as secretary of the Woman's Auxiliary of the National Baptist Convention, Nannie Helen Burroughs said, "We shall work harder than ever for the foreign fields of our church, but let us start a national school for girls here at home ... one that all Negro women, of every creed, can work together on. We don't know what we can do until we all get together and try" (Daniel 1970, p. 111). Fortunately, she was able to realize her dream of a national school for African American girls with a program of hard work. Nannie, the offspring of freedmen, was born May 2, 1883 in Orange, Virginia. She was reared and educated in Washington, D.C., where she finished high school as an honor student in business and domestic science. She obtained further organizational and budgetary skills by working as a bookkeeper, stenographer, and editorial secretary for the Foreign Mission Board of the National Baptist Convention in Louisville, Kentucky.

The ground work for the later development of the national school was done through the organization, supervision, and growth of the Woman's Industrial Club, which Nannie founded. In rental quarters she taught evening classes at the cost of ten cents weekly to each club member interested in learning bookkeeping, sewing, typewriting, millinery, shorthand, cooking, and handicrafts.

Perhaps the immediate experience that led Nannie to establish the school was her election to the secretaryship of the Woman's Auxiliary of the National Baptist Convention in 1900. She moved the thirty-five members from raising fifteen dollars per year to thirteen thousand dollars per year. They organized 14,500 new missionary and educational societies in the United States and missions in South America, Africa, Haiti, and the West Indies. They pleaded the cause of womanhood. It was in this group of women that Miss Burroughs's idea of a national institute was expressed in 1907, and it came into being on October 19, 1909.

With seven girls, six acres of land, an eight-room house in need of repairs standing on an ugly red clay hillside, one assistant, and a $6,500 debt, Nannie Burroughs began to process her dream and teach African American women and girls the essence of clean lives, clean bodies, and clean homes. Because she wanted them to understand the motto, "Wherever you live make that place better" (Daniel 1970, p. 122), she taught at the secondary school level household administration, dining room and dormitory management, laundering, home nursing, printing, art, interior decorating, and business fundamentals.

In order to help with the finances and build good public relations, Mrs. Ella Ewell Whitfield was appointed the full-time responsibility of making friends and raising funds for the school. The positive efforts of Mrs. Whitfield made it possible to add a two-year teacher-training department, two acres of land, a community house, additional staff, and the training of more than 2,500 women from the West Indies, Africa, Central America, and most of the states. The graduates became caterers, teachers, stenographers, dressmakers, insurance agents, housekeepers, beauty specialists, missionaries, milliners, and social workers.

Miss Burroughs believed that African Americans should be the major supporters of their own interests and causes. Therefore, the greater part of collecting funds was done primarily in their communities. All support was gladly accepted, whether it was a postage stamp, dime, dollar, or large sums such as the $3,500 received from the Baptist Home Mission Society.

Nannie Helen Burroughs was an effective administrator because she was a very intelligent woman with specific ideas about what she wanted to do and how to do it. She worked diligently to prove her cause by demonstrating the meaning of theory and practice in the education of women. She provided the leadership to train and explain the meaning of living in capitalist America, where an individual was free to extend a sense of spiritualness for the benefit of all. While Nannie Burroughs's work focused on women, religion, and the community, in no way did this hinder her from becoming nationally known. She spoke out regularly through connections associated with the National Association for the Advancement of Colored People and the Women's Clubs. She was steadfast in her commitment to self-determination, understanding, and the humanness of all people under one god.

Mary McLeod Bethune

The African American woman with the greatest variety of administrative experiences, breadth of influence, leadership opportunities, and power may have been Mary McLeod Bethune, born July 10, 1885 in Mayesville, South Carolina. She spent her childhood years on a rice and cotton farm with her parents in a log cabin. Formal educational experiences began at age eleven in a small Presbyterian mission school, where she won a scholarship to Scotia Seminary in Concord, North Carolina. Because of her friendliness and missionary spirit she was awarded a scholarship to study further at Moody Bible Institute in Chicago. Unable to obtain a missionary appointment to Africa through the Presbyterian Mission Board, she accepted a position to teach in Augusta, Georgia in the Haines Normal and Industrial Institute founded by Lucy Laney.

Returning to her home state, she taught for two years, married Albert

Bethune, and gave birth to a son. She spent an additional five years in mission work in Palatka, Florida until she could no longer resist the drive to build a mission school for African American girls. With one dollar and fifty cents, her small son, a rented cabin issued to her on faith, dry goods boxes, and courage, Mary McLeod Bethune opened the Daytona Educational Industrial Training School with five female pupils on October 4, 1904 in Daytona Beach, Florida on a dump called Hell's Hole. Upon this spot an instituition developed with a board of trustees, a secretary, a treasurer, and a charter to do business from the state of Florida. With steady progress for more than fifteen years, the Institute obtained state and national recognition.

The board of education of the Methodist Episcopal Church, which controlled the Cookman Institute in Jacksonville, Florida, was so impressed that they agreed to merge with Daytona Institute in July 1923 as a new school for females and males. It was to be called Bethune Cookman College, and Mrs. Bethune was to be President. One of the unusual ways used to obtain support and friends for the college was to search the newspapers for names of prominent whites vacationing in Florida. Mrs. Bethune would write and request an opportunity to speak with them. James N. Gamble of Proctor and Gamble Company became a generous friend by this means and aided the rapid growth of the college (Lerner 1973).

Under her leadership the institution became an accredited college with thirty staff persons to work with somewhat less than three hundred students. The beautiful campus housed fourteen well-structured buildings on thirty-two acres of land. When Mrs. Bethune learned that there was no hospital available to African Americans for a 200-mile stretch from Daytona Beach, she immediately provided one room with one bed in the college for that purpose. This later developed into a structure of twenty-six beds and accompanying offices, and it became known as the McLeod Hospital and Training School for Nurses for almost twenty years. She also developed an Evening Opportunity School, Young Women's and Men's Christian Associations, and a goodwill interracial center for the state of Florida. In addition, Mrs. Bethune provided leadership to the nation in wartime and afterward. She was founder of the Negro War Relief of New York City, speaker for the Red Cross, President of the National Association of Teachers in Colored Schools and the National Association of Colored Women, and she assisted in forming the National Council of Negro Women.

In 1930 President Herbert Hoover invited Mrs. Bethune to assist with the White House Conference on Child Health and Protection. President Franklin D. Roosevelt asked her to serve on the Advisory Committee of the National Youth Administration. One year later she was made Director of the Division of Negro Affairs; she served in this position for eight years (Daniel 1970). She served as special assistant to the Secretary of War in the selection of African American officer candidates to serve in the Women's Auxiliary Corps. Her combined leadership roles in these various government programs resulted in the participation of more than 800,000 African American youth in educational activities (Ploski and Warren II 1976). Mrs. Bethune also served as the only female member of the unofficial "Black Cabinet," which served as the forerunner to the desegregation process in the federal government.

Mary McLeod Bethune received the Springarn Award in 1935 for her work in the area of brotherhood, the Frances A. Drexel award for service to African Americans, and the Thomas Jefferson Medal for excellent leadership in 1942. She died in 1955. In 1974 a $400,000 memorial monument to her was opened to the public in Lincoln Park. This monument was the first built to honor an African American person or a woman on the soil of Washington, D.C. (Ploski and Warren II 1976). She should be remembered as an able leader and administrator who possessed a pleasant nature with an urge and willingness to learn and prepare for tentative goals. Mrs. Bethune demonstrated the ability and enthusiasm to serve when bold opportunities were presented. From childhood she radiated adoration from family and friends and was unafraid to use the heart in guiding programs and people. She was a likeable person acceptable to most because of her decency as a human being.

THE LEGACY

African American women administrators from the past have demonstrated many human values and practical skills in their efforts to build educational experiences and gain equity with other ethnic groups in America. It may be that many of their ways and means can be equally useful today as African American women continue to seek equity in the developing atmosphere of diversity. These women should be highly regarded since their endeavors and accomplishments took place during a time when enormous odds against their acceptance as American citizens were far more difficult to overcome than today. In those days an abundance of anti-African American attitudes were evident in cultural customs and the laws enforced by the white power structure in general throughout the United States. In addition, there were hostile beatings and burnings, which it was acceptable for whites to brag about. Much of this evilness took place in some of the Southern states where most of the schools founded by these women were located. Not only were these women following a dream, but they were very brave to attempt their ventures in the presence of such violence, even with the help of friends.

These female front-runners encountered an abundance of ignorance from all facets of educational, political, and economic life. Ignorance was used as an excuse for the uselessness of sharing resources on individuals believed to be incapable of learning. This same myth was believed by many of the unfortunate ones affected. Their self-concept was so reduced that they accepted a servant-of-servant status as a normal life expectation. It was a stupendous task to become knowledgeable about the societal system while at the same time beginning to believe positively in and know themselves as part of that system. Few people were willing and prepared to assist with this cause. Yet these women faced the issues and requirements, and they built the necessary institutions where these concepts could become part of the educational process.

Their model was determined ages ago by their ancient sisters and was extended to them through a spiritual sense of sisterhood. Women from the ancient past provided guidance, organized, and managed responsibilities for the sake of the group so they could survive as a cooperating unit. They expressed a sense of the female self in organizing and managing affairs to care for the development of the young. When it was necessary they were prepared to manage and give leadership to the affairs of state or kingdom. They developed trade routes to support an economy, and they provided protection by heading an army to fight for what was valued. These things and many others could not have been done without women knowing how to do "things" with order, feelings, and a sense of empowerment.

The women of the recent past were not too different from their ancestors in giving meaning and direction to efforts that were valued. They, too, understood togetherness, sharing, and cooperation. These women of the late 1800s and 1900s understood they had all the freedom to follow their vision because they believed, had confidence, and were committed to a strong sense of self-help and direction. Their common interest was to build institutions for the development of African American women. They each possessed a compelling ideal and little or no financial support. The families from which they came were relatively poor but offered help nonetheless. They were able to maintain a steady support system with their Christian faith, church missions, women's clubs, and a sense of peoplehood. One of their major goals was to build character in women by emphasizing in their institutional programs the quality of mind, health, and manners. These women were highly ambitious, possessed great energy and courage, and understood the meaning of sacrifice. They were skillful in building goodwill, which was needed for acquiring help and raising funds. They learned how to work with all kinds of people from the rich and powerful white friends and donors to the eager and ordinary common people of the streets. They were aware that there must be a state of community consciousness to which accountability was notable and to which the givers of nickels and dimes could feel they

belonged. These administrators understood that humans had their im-
perfections but that builders of educational institutions could not afford
to shut themselves off from the vast resources of our dynamic society
and expect to grow and develop to the fullest.

These model leaders and managers have also handed down to their
present-day sisters a commonsense ethic to work hard without the fear
of making a mistake or feeling ashamed to ask for help. In all cases their
success came from many positive experiences along with many hours
of worry and toil when it often appeared that no answer was apparent
to solve their problem. Although prayer was part of the process, it took
patience, compassion, and intelligence to solve the many problems that
faced them.

African American women cannot afford to live in the past because the
world of today demands that they be prepared for rapid change. History
suggests that women cannot afford to forego the challenge of their
inheritance that suggests that sharing is one of the most effective ways
of acquiring leadership potential. Although the word "mentor" had not
been used, mentoring has been with them in one way or another over
the ages. Many management skills have been taught by grandmama,
mama, aunts, cousins, and neighbors who mentored by the system of
"just watch me and do as I do, if you want to learn something, girl."
Lucy C. Laney mentored Mary McLeod Bethune, along with several
other women. It is within the province of many more women to share
meaningful skills, even though at times such service may appear to be
unappreciated by the ones being helped. Therefore, in this process it is
worth considering the persons to be involved. There should be some
indication of a degree of respect, decency, and likeableness to promote
the experience of mentoring. There should be enough interest and caring
to support a willingness to give and accept criticism. An understanding
should prevail that there must be an energy level to promote the development of tasks that can be shared and learned. When there is evidence of harmony with the personalities and responsibilities involved,
it is reasonable to expect successful mentoring to take place.

In many ways women with administrative skills can mentor and assist
in developing future managers and administrators in all areas of higher
education. One can serve as a teacher for a particular woman by assisting
in the improvement of her interpersonal skills. Give feedback on what
has been done and suggest different ways to approach the same problem. Use one's position in an institution to facilitate the entry of a bright,
striving woman into an administrative position. A seasoned administrator could introduce an aspiring woman to influential people and share
with her the values and culture of the institution. A senior administrator
might mentor by being available to provide advice and offer moral support when a crisis situation exists. Being visible at functions sponsored

by women is a way for African American women presidents, vice presidents, and other upper-level administrators to serve as an inspiration. By using these and other mentoring opportunities, African American women in higher education administration will continue to use their legacy as a resource for future generations of young women.

Today, many African American women have heard and are busy following their legacy from the past. A few present-day college presidents are Johnnetta Cole, Spelman College, Atlanta, Georgia; Niara Sudarkasa, Lincoln University, Lincoln, Pennsylvania; Gloria Scott, Bennett College, Greensboro, North Carolina; Constance Carroll, Saddleback College, Mission Viejo, California; Vera King Farris, Stockton State College, Pomona, New Jersey; Brenda Wilson, University of Michigan, Dearborn, Michigan; and, most recently, Marquerite Ross Barnett was appointed President of the University of Houston, Houston, Texas (Office of Women in Higher Education, List of 1987 Minority Presidents). Numerous black women are serving on boards of higher education and are working in administrative positions as deans, vice presidents, directors, department heads, and managers of various departments. In addition, there are professional organizations such as the National Association of Women Deans, Administrators, and Counselors; the American Council on Education, National Identification Program; the Bryn Mawr Summer Institute for Women in Higher Education Administration; and the Smith College Management Institute and Black Women in Higher Education Administration—these all offer programs to assist women in acquiring appropriate skills for administrative roles in higher education. Women may refine their management skills by reading the books *Paths to Power* by Natasha Josefowitz and *Power of the Presidency* by James L. Fisher.

From the purity of womanhood represented by Isis to the heritable inferences relative to organizational knowledge and skills from the ancient mothers, African American women must feel proud that their group and society are better because of their administrative and leadership efforts of sharing, inspiring, and encouraging a high sense of competence, responsibility, and practical values. The legacy is ever before us to continue the challenge through our higher education pursuits.

5

The Ultimate Negotiation: Communication Challenges for African American Women in Higher Education

Mary Ann Williams

Every good academician worth his/her keep begins with a definition of terms. I will take the liberty to create my own combination of words to describe the thoughts and feelings of today's women of color. What is the ultimate negotiation? A round peg and square hole convincing each other to shave off an inch here and there so they can fit together snugly when it's time to move. And it is now movin' day.

What are communication challenges? These challenges are the "how to's" of surviving with as much joy as one can wrestle from life, and as much dignity as time and talent permit. All the ol' sisters through time from the banks of the Nile and the shores of Barbados, to the front porches of Plain City, Ohio and the balconies and stoops of New York City lower their voices as they pass on the pain of their "communication challenges" to their blood and nonblood daughters and granddaughters.

Who are African American women? They are the Eve of the 1990s. They have all the rights of failure and the responsibilities of success that accompany being the first of anything.

What is higher eduation? Higher education is the courage one acquires during the rites of passage. Higher education begins in the Sisterhood Department, which is part of the College of Humankind, a subdivision of the University of the Spirit.

What is the purpose of this study? The purpose is to tap the resources in our history, homes, and hearts while meeting today's leadership crisis. Marian Anderson, the world's first African American Metropolitan Opera vocalist, and 1958 alternate delegate to the United Nations, once said that leadership should be born out of the understanding of the needs of those who would be affected by it.

By example, African American women must lead themselves, their families, the nation, and the world into a more flexible, forgiving future that includes basic fairness and less foolishness. This chapter gives examples of some successful and less successful negotiations of African American women who are responding to the challenges of leadership.

When I interviewed Dr. Laura Shepard, recently the Information Services Director for the Ohio State University Libraries, for her viewpoint on communication challenges she had experienced, she asked, "Are we going to do this interview in a formal fashion or are we going to do what we do best—just talk?" Communication had begun on a sister-to-sister, tell-it-like-it-is basis, with no "negotiation" necessary and no time for extra formalities even if it were. Mrs. Mildred Welch, also known as Mom Millie of Columbus's Hanford Village, and my deceased great aunt Ida would call this kind of negotiation "turnin' and twistin.' " So I'll talk without too much turnin' and twistin.'

I'll share some, not all, of what I've learned about the challenges of quadruple jeopardy: being black, female, educated, and isolated. This discussion demands a candid look at the day-to-day challenges of African American women's survival in higher education. The African American women's communication challenges are as follows: (1) how to keep the heart in humanity and (2) how to pass through life leaving a mark that is not a deep, deep scar.

If they choose a career in academia, all African American women must negotiate with the system, within the system, and with themselves to determine how they will control their actions, words, thoughts, and feelings on a moment-to-moment basis.

In academia, the level of education plays little or no role in an African American woman's communication challenges. Her primary responsibility in the communications process is to control when she is, or is not, "heard." If she is a masterful "negotiator" she will be in control of herself when Murphy's Law goes into effect. Murphy says anything that can go wrong will go wrong. In my "African American Woman's Communicator's Handbook," Murphy is the white Eshu. In African mythology, the Yoruba tribe's Eshu is a trickster whose greatest joy is to keep people frustrated, fuming, and fussing. Eshu's costume adds to his diversionary powers. His cape and other clothing is one-half red and one-half black. Eshu always positions himself so that no two people will see the same side of him simultaneously; consequently, people can never agree on the nature of Eshu. They lose sight of whatever their original purpose for communicating was as they debate whether Eshu is dressed in red or black. Eshu gets in the middle of African American women when they are negotiating life. He dons the educator's role, confusing all concerned.

Education is the trickster's tool for fooling African American women (and men) into believing there is a difference between "glass ceiling" or "Glass Plus." In academia, the glass ceiling is a silent, invisible barrier to one's upward mobility in the professorial and administrative ranks. As a former professional cleaning woman, I recommend Glass Plus as THE best window-cleaning agent, surpassing Windex or the old standby, vinegar and newspaper.

Both the formally educated and the "experience-wise" must understand that their existence depends on their recognizing and respecting the glass barrier that impedes them. They must clearly see themselves in it, clean or care for it properly, and break through it, if it begins to suffocate them. Survival is the first and only law of nature. Education, Eshu, or Glass Plus notwithstanding, African American women must communicate their intentions, needs, and desires. They cannot stand on protocol or prayer alone. They must use any means necessary, available, and practical to ensure their survival with joy.

As the only African American faculty person to serve as a Presidential Intern at the Ohio State University (OSU), I had to redefine survival in academia. The opportunity to be a participant-observer in Dr. Edward H. Jennings's administration, office staff, and cabinet was a close encounter with the best raw power can offer. The administrators, faculty, and students in this billion-dollar institution of approximately 59,000 students and 22,000 staff are amazingly efficient, outwardly funless, deliberately fearless, and often fierce. Adjusting to the presence of an African American forty-ish female from a communication arts background in a technical thinker's world was a learning experience for all concerned. Were there communication challenges? Yes, one or two. I had to move from the world of highly verbal interaction with students in the classroom and with colleagues in Black Studies and the College of Humanities into the relatively nonverbal administrative realms. The interaction was much more subtle than the experience I had had as Acting Chairperson of the Department of Black Studies the previous year.

Talking was not at all the way in which anything of substance was communicated. In a white male world, with a few white women in influential positions, an African American woman needed to find a way to communicate, quietly. Early on I observed these communication patterns:

1. Men stand in groups and talk openly about what may appear to some as nothing but the weather and sports, when they really are communicating

enormous information by the conversation partner, position in the room, distance from the person of power, or arrival time at the pre-meeting rituals. Women do not stand anywhere for too long.

2. Men walk in a leisurely manner to the rest room. Women walk fast everywhere, especially to and from the rest room.

Rest rooms are actually power places for women as well as men. I felt the most invisible and powerless in the common area of the dreary first-floor rest room. In many powder rooms women occasionally exchange inanities. In this rest room, the business rhythm was continuous.

It was during the first week of my six-month internship that I met an African American housekeeping person in the administration building who had served the university for decades. She was cleaning the rest room mirror when I walked into the semi-crowded room at lunch time. All the women were as relaxed as one gets in close proximity to strangers. The cleaning person and I acknowledged each other with a respectful nod as the others chatted. I thought I noticed that somehow she was not in their conscious presence, nor was I for that matter. As weeks passed, the power powder room observation was confirmed.

This housekeeping person was Ralph Ellison's Invisible Woman prototype and I felt invisible along with her. The patrons' denying her humanity took away from mine. She focused on each task, for example, mirror, floor, waste can, whatever, but she was constantly aware of the activity in her surroundings.

Once the cleaning woman and I talked briefly about my being a speaker at her church on Women's Day sometime. I was as honored by this as I had been to be invited to be one of the President's participant-observers. My polite two-minute exchange with the housekeeping person paralleled the cabinet members' pre-meeting ritual conversations. The real subject was

1. Positioning—to acknowledge our sisterhood without verbalizing it.
2. Focusing—on the need for a communication of spirits in our home and work lives.
3. Listening—to the even, deliberate speech patterns that reflected the superficial calm of the administrative milieu.
4. Revealing—as little of significance as possible.

In the President's office everybody was cool, communicating with class—casually, cautiously, and sometimes caustically. Observing the Invisible Woman one could add "calmly carefree" to the descriptions. She kept her priorities straight and her mirror image polished to Glass Plus perfection.

The Invisible Woman communicated tremendous personal power.

One saw her dignity in her erect posture, neatly pressed and carefully worn uniform; her pride in punctuality; and the pleasure she derived from sweeping, dusting, and mopping well. Rumor had it that she had been instructed to do the marble staircase on her hands and knees until the past three years. In my professional cleaning days thirty years ago, scrubbing on hands and knees was like today's rallying cry, "I don't do windows."

When possible, the housekeeping person brought the OSU campus papers upstairs each morning for the convenience of the President's staff. This was beyond the duties of her job description but she admired, as I did, the President and his hard-working support team. The Invisible Woman and some of the office staff had developed respect for each other over the years.

Respect is difficult to come by when it is perceived as a "power chip" and not a natural right of all human beings, like the right to breathe. The Invisible Woman had earned this respect with few words and consistent, hard work. The Invisible Woman had the African American's dream: personal power.

Members of the President's cabinet also had personal power in varying degrees. Those who used it with restraint were the most effective communicators. These cabinet people provided me the opportunity to talk and work with their staffs.

I focused much of my time on reviewing and interpreting the OSU Office of Finance's communication process during the cost containment initiatives. The Office of Finance communicates so much information so quickly that it is easy for the shorthand of language to short-circuit effective communications. According to the Vice President of Finance, my report was the most candid and useful analysis of the cost containment program thus far. He said my recommendation to change the language and thought patterns of cost containment from impersonal words like "units" to more humanistic terms like "people" was extremely useful. I was gratified when he discussed the "units" to "people" terminology in his Faculty Senate speech that reviewed the cost containment program.

Contributing to this speech may seem a minor point; but as a staff person, it was a major experience for me in team playing. I had seen my research become a part of policy considerations. My experience in academia as an African American female was largely "alone and toughing it out," as a white female colleague once observed. Having influence as a team member rather than limited personal power was an extremely unusual occurrence in my negotiations in higher education.

LET'S DO LUNCH AND MORE

The African American woman in higher education is rare. The reasons for this are many, but some undeniable factors are the layers of verbal,

nonverbal, and extra-verbal language that she must translate instanta-
neously and adeptly in negotiating her existence and future in academia.

What does "Let's do lunch" mean to an African American woman in
academia? She must ask all the following questions and more:

1. Does this mean I am being asked to "break bread" in the context of my
   culture?
2. Do I have to diffuse all the stereotypes of African American people by definitely not ordering chicken or watermelon?
3. Is it safe to wear something red without being thought of as related to Sap-
   phire, an argumentative siren, and not former First Lady Nancy Reagan?
4. Am I being checked out as a potential "team" member?
5. Will I be mistaken for a secretary to my white female or male colleague again?
6. If any or all of these or more happens, how will I remain calm and move
   past the situation? If I show any reactions, I will be accused of being too
   sensitive or radical.

This list is only one of many such examples of negotiation that African
American women must perform adeptly on a daily basis in academia.

Dr. Anne Pruitt, Professor of Educational Policy and Leadership and
Director of the Center for Teaching Excellence at OSU, told this story
about watermelon:

I was having lunch with a colleague one day, a white male dean who is no
longer here at OSU. He was my host and was typically writing out the chit. I
ordered the fruit salad, without the watermelon. I can't eat watermelon. It
doesn't agree with me. I wish I could quote him but he said something to the
effect that "I thought all black people liked watermelon." This is a perfect example of someone being honest and candid and not meaning to be offensive.
He just thought that was the way it was.

Dr. Pruitt did not confront the person because she thought it was not
worth the effort at that time. She did directly address the following
incident. Dr. Pruitt continued:

Sometimes things happen to us that are not as blatant as that [incident] but that
we interpret as being racist. I am on the board of trustees at Case Western
Reserve University in Cleveland, Ohio. And when I go to the meetings, there
is a special parking place that is normally used by everybody; but on the days
of our meetings, it is blocked off.

When I drove up to the gate where the guard was, he said, "This is reserved
for trustees today." I said, "I'm a trustee." He said, "What is your name?" And
he had to go to a list and find my name on the list. He had not done this for
any of the other trustees. They simply said, "I am a trustee" and they had driven
on through.

So I didn't say anything to him because I didn't see any reason to talk to him. I talked to the President of Case Western Reserve. This is an instance where I did confront it. I told him exactly what happened and that they needed some sensitivity training for their traffic and parking people. He was very apologetic. This is a case when I did not ignore it.

Dr. Pruitt pinpointed two key steps for effective communication: (1) She addressed her comments to someone she knew could make a difference, and (2) she gave the person specific recommendations for actions he could take. Dr. Pruitt went on to state:

I felt that saying something to the young man would not have made a difference. Nothing would have happened. He may have learned something personally, but I felt that the impact should be greater and that the impact needed to go to the entire traffic and parking force.

I am giving my time to Case Western University and I thought the University President should know of that instance. I said to him, "Now you can understand how the students and the faculty on this campus feel. These things are still going on." I had quite a lengthy talk with him about it.

Dr. Pruitt encourages and advises African American women in academia to proceed with care:

First of all, I think you have to understand "the system." Those are code words for what I am talking about, but I think you understand. You have to understand the power relationships. How the system operates. You have to be highly regarded yourself. And in order to do that, it means what we have always known and always been taught. To be a woman and particularly an African American woman you have to be better than the next person and have to have done more than the next person just to be regarded as equal.

You have to be pretty clear in understanding who you are and how that system regards who you are. You have to have a certain amount of confidence and security in order to take the consequences of whatever that may be.

To have this communication that I have just shared with you, I had to say to myself that it didn't make any difference. The President of Case Western could have said that he didn't want Anne Pruitt on that board. Although I doubted that would happen, I had to say to myself that it didn't make any difference to be on that board and for them to know who I was. I did the right thing. If you want to translate that into implications for actions in other settings, those key characteristics are: feel secure, confident, and do your homework.

Homework takes a lot of listening. Interactions. A lot of participation. It's very time consuming. It's doing things. Being on committees and being on boards that you probably would rather not be on. It requires networking. We did not know what that term meant a few years ago. Know who the people are with whom you can share confidences. Most of them you can't share, but you learn it the hard way.

You've got to secure some mentors. You have them for various reasons. All of this helps you to test the waters. To let you know if you ought to be feeling as confident, have more security than you think you have. Or how you obtain that security. So you know what's going on. So that when you have to take a stand, you know that you are not going to fall on your face.

I asked Dr. Pruitt how mentors are obtained and about networking. She replied:

There are vibes that you get. You don't find this in the literature at all. It's just like developing friendships. Sometimes you like people instantly and they like you. Sometimes you cultivate these friendships. A mentor doesn't have to be an older person. It can be somebody who has had an experience you haven't had and is willing to share it with you. A person who has an outlook and perspective on the work, or life, or the world that broadens your own perspective and a person who is willing to interpret you to yourself. To tell you how you are seen, to advise you on how you might not want to be seen or how you would rather be seen. It has to be one who isn't going to play games with you.

When I asked about those times when one does take a stand and falls flat on her face, Dr. Pruitt sighed gently as if she were reviewing a painful moment in her illustrious career. She carefully added, "It is hard. Pick yourself up and start all over."

POWER PAUSE

Mom Millie in Hanford Village would say, "You've got to take just a *minute* to 'blow a bit.' " I have observed that the successful African American women, in whatever capacity in higher education, take "assessment seconds," not a minute. People often perceive these seconds as a sign of uncertainty or lethargy. These descriptions could be the 80's and 90's euphemisms for "shiftless" and "lazy."

There are definitely cultural linkages that tie African American women with a more Afrocentric point of view to a personal communication style that is reflective and deliberate. Many African cultures require an acknowledgment of all ancestors, customs, and other factors. This takes time. These amenities result in a leisurely pace that some mistake for "being too slow" or "not having what it takes." The academic euphemism is "There isn't a fit."

When a male, particularly a white male, pauses a few seconds, he is "reflecting." Depending on his perceived power, the listeners may wait respectfully as he "gathers his thoughts." When a woman pauses, she is perceived as "hesitating" or "being indecisive." This diminishes her power as an effective communicator and leader.

The pause in nonverbal communication is powerful. Silence often makes people uncomfortable. They rush to fill it with words, laughter, coughs, shuffling of papers, moving of chairs, or sometimes fidgeting imperceptibly.

As a TV/radio producer and host and solo performer, I had to negotiate the planned or unplanned pause. Interviewees or performers on "Afromation," the one-half hour weekly, three-time Emmy nominated program on WOSU-TV taught me well. During its six-year run, I learned to anticipate the nature of the pause by listening carefully to the technical speech patterns (rate, pitch, tone, etc.) of the guests while staying riveted to the content of the conversation.

Effective communication was dependent upon my negotiating the guests' uses of the pause. Many of the professionals on the media circuits made my job easy, since communication was their business. They added their own rhythms to the program. Unfortunately, people in the early 70's simply did not know how to use the media. Academics in the early days of broadcasting sometimes failed to pause for exchange with other guests. Being a young African American female, I found it difficult to keep communication flowing and not appear rude. The expectations of public TV and radio audiences were quite different then. Confrontation was not the norm.

COMMUNICATION CHALLENGES
IN THE CLASSROOM

The most exciting part of working in higher education is greeting the energy, enthusiasm, and enormous anxiety of the students who need the best one can give.

Students challenge professors to give them their money's worth (or a grade that made sitting through the class or showing up for the final exam worthwhile). Challenges come in many forms. They are certainly a function of race, gender, and subject area. Students/people assume that a male math/science/business professor (white or black) will know his subject area and be involved in "serious" work. A white female will often experience some resistance, but a certain level of competence can be presumed.

As an African American female (with a smile) and an arts background, I encounter a "you have got to be kidding" look that takes over the students' faces when I enter a classroom. Most white males and females distrust the African American woman's knowledge base and certainly feel a need to challenge her authority.

Most students regardless of color and gender have not had the opportunity to experience formalized instruction with African American professionals. Too often, OSU students' only prior experience with African American women is with housekeepers, workers at entry-level summer jobs, or a few school mates. Many people of color also have limited experience with African American female professionals. Students often see the female professor as a mother figure, TV mammy, or real-life nanny, although many OSU students have had exposure to African American professional women in their churches or schools.

Most OSU students simply don't know what to expect. The first three weeks of class many students spend "whitening me up." The longer I stand before the students, the more I become "just like them." "People are people!" they say. Yet I am instant Ovaltine/Nestlé Quik mix as I begin to teach the beauty of *Sally Hemings*, the story of President Thomas Jefferson's slave mistress, by author Barbara Chase Riboud. Even though I display the same fervor in classes about Maxine Hong Kingston's *Woman Warrior* or Carlos Castaneda's *Journey to Ixtlan*, suddenly "people are *not* people"; and I become one of "you people" to most of my students.

I am now "black" in their eyes again. Many say they are "uncomfortable." To their credit as dedicated learners, most get past themselves into the new experience of taking on a different perspective. They don't always make it; but they try.

The students' youthful energy keeps me going, even when I weary of their stereotypic impressions of me. To communicate effectively, the students and I have to thoughtfully bridge the gaps between us with caring and sharing. Although I think I may initiate the negotiations and the "giving" too frequently, the students fortunately grow in spite of my errors.

At the conclusion of my internship with Dr. Edward H. Jennings, I returned to a classroom assignment. Despite my objections, my chairperson assured me that my teaching assignment would be a snap. The "snap" was Black Studies 101, which met Monday through Friday at the peak hour of 11:00 a.m. to noon. This basic education requirement course had 140 undergraduate students enrolled in it.

Since I had never taught a class larger than 60 students, I knew there was only one way out: revel in my administrative dreams of grandeur and forget the impending nightmare. Rumor had it that the Caucasian first-year students who usually constituted the majority of students in the Black Studies 101 class expected an "easy A." These students reputedly proved the only mathematical certainty I could conjure, "Nothing from nothing leaves nothing."

As the Presidential Intern, I had become accustomed to the pace and communication patterns of the upper-level administrative team. When I walked into Black Studies 101, I was astounded that some students barely knew there was a president of Ohio State University, to say nothing of his intern. I had not been in the classroom in two years; students had changed and so had I. The students were rawer, leaner, meaner, and deceptively cleaner. Short haircuts on men were not the "clean cut" of the 50's and 60's but a sign of the skinhead or neo-Nazi.

These students were not preoccupied with the pursuit of learning, but rather the pursuit of the American dollar or anybody else's. They "scoped out" the professor of any class by what the professor could do to get them closer to Yuppie (Young Upwardly Mobile Professional) or Buppie (Black Upwardly Mobile Professional) Heaven. Sixty percent of the 140 students were Caucasian and the other 40 percent were African Americans.

Students love testing professors; it is part of their rite of passage. These students were no exception. My twenty years in the classroom and my executive training signaled the need for an offensive move, immediately. Since effective communication can begin with a person's name, I requested pictures of every student in the class and learned the names as quickly as possible. Soon the huge class had a small-group interaction mode as opposed to the impersonal lecture hall syndrome. People chatted comfortably with each other and with me.

The class was laughing at something in my lecture and one of the robust white males in the back of the hall yelled down to me, "Yeah, Baby, that's right!" I removed my rose-colored rimmed glasses (which was the ultimate of body language for my fifth grade teacher, Mrs. Merrill) and said, "Sir, it is *Doctor* Williams. I save 'Baby' for *MY* man!" There was a silence in the hall, then a huge burst of laughter and scattered applause.

I discovered that the young man who was too "familiar" was one of the many football players in the class. At OSU being a football player carries great prestige among the many students and the 90,000 regular stadium fans. These athletes intimidate many professors and students by their size, influence, and attitudes.

This young white male came to my office later in the quarter. He unceremoniously shut the door when he entered. This man was indeed formidable. He had a huge neck and weighed well over 225 pounds. I envisioned being crushed into the lock of my filing cabinet as revenge for the applause I had received when I reminded him I was an African American female professor who did not want to be disrespected by being called "Baby."

My fears were totally ill-founded. This junior student came to tell me that until he took my class he had read only one complete book in his entire education. That book was *Catcher in the Rye* by Salinger, and he wanted me to know that he had finished his second book, *Jubilee* by Margaret Walker. I was delighted that an African American woman's historical novel about a female slave and her Civil War experiences had awakened this white student's desire to learn and to read. After he had completed *Jubilee* he said he no longer felt dumb. He had already started reading the next assignment, *Brothers* by Sylvester Monroe and Peter Goldman. The African American mothers in *Brothers* who lived in the projects reminded the student of his mom who had adopted him. My student-athlete-scholar related to the mothers in *Brothers* who were religious and hardworking like his waitress mom.

Later in the quarter, one of OSU's academic advisors for football shared more of the now scholar-athlete's story. Dysfunctional white families, like black ones, do produce excellent human beings. The common human experience in *Jubilee* and *Brothers* had communicated hope to this young man.

Months later I again saw this scholar-athlete. He was at an appreciation cookout that the Department of Athletics sponsors annually for supporters of their programs and the athletes. He had been injured in practice and was on crutches. He said he had hobbled over from his dorm, hoping I'd be there. He introduced me to his roommate as "Doc Williams, the prof I made the mistake of calling 'Baby'." The roommate and I both laughed. We were all three communicating effectively and in the common language of the heart, laughter, and mutual respect.

SPIRIT DRAMA SOCIETY

African American female students at the Ohio State University must find alternative means for validating their past and presenting their present goals to the university community. These students must justify every aspect of their lives from the dormitory to the classroom. Insensitive and uninformed roommates and residence hall advisors too frequently ridicule and harrass these women for their dress, hair and hair care, music, and men.

When African American women attend classes, many professors see "problems" rather than receptive young minds in different colored bodies. They often presume the following about these women:

1. They are not capable of doing the work.
2. They are taking scholarship money from accomplished students.
3. They are products of the welfare system.
4. They are "illegitimate" children and have one or more "bastards" of their own.

The campus, university area, and the greater Columbus, Ohio community reflect American society's reckless disregard and hostility for the well-being of African American women. Student status does not exempt any of these women from being indiscriminately physically and verbally abused at an alarming rate; consequently, they must always be aware of casual insults and/or looming dangers.

At OSU there is little time and few places for most of these women to experience a total college life of facts, fun, and fellowship. Negotiating the communication challenges in their dormitory rooms, classrooms, and the campus and community environments is like traversing an endless mine field with OSU graduation barely in sight. Any error or lapse in judgment could cause physical or mental devastation not only for them but also for many other African American students, staff, and faculty who have accepted the challenges inherent in crossing the "mind" field. The communication challenges African American women students face at OSU require an investment on the part of African American female faculty and other professional women to serve as role models, mentors, and confidants for their academic, social, and spiritual lives.

African American culture does not traditionally separate these facets of personal development; therefore, many of these women expect a different level of concern from the OSU faculty and administrative personnel. The Afrocentric perspective assumes that the whole person (including mind, body, and spirit) is carefully considered at all times. Most Eurocentrically oriented Americans compartmentalize education and all other aspects of their existence. Many resist and/or refuse to share with students any knowledge beyond their certified area of concentration. They find any need for a holistic learning approach to be an unrealistic expectation.

My experience as a master's student in the OSU Department of Theatre in 1971–1972 was a walking nightmare. The isolation was indescribable and the opportunities for performance or directing were nonexistent. I opted for a focus in literary criticism because no other realistic avenue existed for a woman of color. As the first African American woman (or perhaps, person) in the department since the 1950s, I was quite a novelty. Few people initiated interactions with me, personally or professionally.

My saving grace was the support, direction, and love from my master's degree committee, Dr. Ojo Arewa from the Department of Anthropology, Dr. Lynn Morrow from the Division of Comparative Studies, and Lynn's extensive cadre of professional liaisons at OSU. This unconventional Caucasian soul sister kept me focused on my strengths and potential. Through her consistent, constructive feedback, I became proficient at discerning my personal growth issues from the deeply embedded racism at OSU.

Upon reflection, I am much more empathetic with the position of the faculty, staff, and administrators during my 1970s graduate studies. On the entire OSU campus, the first African American assistant professor was hired only in the 1950s. By the 1970s the white faculty and staff still had few African American colleagues to assist them in developing appropriate academic, financial, and social support systems for African American students.

Even though my grade point average for my undergraduate work at Wilmington College in Wilmington, Ohio was quite good and I was a native Ohioan, I received no financial aid at OSU. Until the 1980s the University's initiatives for minority student recruitment and financial aid were primarily directed toward black colleges in the South.

Many African American Ohio students were caught in an untenable situation. Their tax dollars and state resources were not readily available to them for graduate or undergraduate education. To object to the University's priorities would have been counterproductive to unity within the African American culture and communities. Yet in private African American circles, this old Columbus adage was passed among the women in particular: "Columbus is the best run plantation in America. Know it, but don't show it." Over the years when American female students' frustrations peaked, I shared that thought with them to help them focus on where they were and how carefully and courageously they had to proceed. Even today the Columbus African American community residents, in particular, have quite an uphill struggle to acquire educational opportunities that should be automatic. Outstanding athletes or honors students, male or female, are priority recruits nationwide; but the good (but not great) academic students still must work the same inordinate number of hours and years to finance their education as I did in the 1960s and 1970s.

In 1978, several dedicated students, Columbus community residents, and I founded the Spirit Drama Society as a formalized, constructive way to address their many needs. Spirit members channeled their energy and frustrations into producing, writing, and directing their original artistic expressions. Spirit members developed specific artistic skills that transferred into their daily lives. They communicated more effectively with each other and their audiences through musicals, dramas, and environmental art performances that evolved from personal experiences.

Spirit Drama Society had these initial goals:

1. To provide opportunities for minority students in the visual and performing arts to develop new skills and sharpen old ones.

2. To provide a public forum or showcase for the original scripts and choreography of Spirit Drama Society and the Black Arts Society.

3. To develop a professional atmosphere within the group that would carry over to their artistic and personal lives.

4. To expose the Society's members to professionals in the arts as role models and potential mentors.

5. To reinforce the necessity for an African American aesthetic as the guiding principle for artistic integrity.

6. To provide the financial and social support for minority women to explore and develop their artistic capabilities.

Although these goals were the primary focus, the Spirit Drama Society's members also addressed these goals:

1. To gain or reclaim their self-respect.

2. To experience positive reinforcement for their artistic expressions and for themselves. They wanted to be appreciated by their peers on campus and in the larger community.

3. To be evaluated on the merit of their contributions and not be arbitrarily dismissed from consideration for performance activities or campus leadership positions or roles.

4. To build a network of support to enable them to achieve academically and graduate.

5. To improve the image of OSU in order to attract other minority students.

6. To establish positive relationships with the Columbus community, especially the minority arts professionals.

7. To market the Spirit Drama Society's productions in order to raise funds for future productions.

8. To present positive images of African American people to the university community.

9. To be happy.

By working side by side, the socially and culturally diverse membership developed mutual respect, support, and admiration.

In the late 1980s, many students, particularly the African American women, were unable to adjust to the whiteness of campus life. Spirit Drama Society activities on and off campus gave members a sense of comfort and belonging. They could relax and be themselves. Even using "Black English" was all right during the Spirit segment of their hectic lives. They communicated their hopes, dreams, frustrations, and future plans with confidence that their peers would validate them and their creative expressions. All Spirit students—gender, race, and sex notwithstanding—were empowered as they participated in developing original theatrical works.

The cohesive philosophy of Spirit was the black aesthetic, which insists upon artistic expressions that reflect self-respect foremost. Spirit's interpretation of the black aesthetic also insisted on tolerance for divergent points of view. This black aesthetic has grounded many young people as they struggled to survive at OSU. In the thirteen years of Spirit's existence, it has maintained a high standard for creative expression; despite this quality work, all departments have consistently denied Spirit access to traditional theatre spaces on the campus. Nonetheless, Spirit continued to do good creative works with great dignity.

Until recently, Spirit's strongest members were African American women. One female Spirit president and I received two university affirmative action grants. These grants supported production costs and workshops with African American visual and performing arts professionals. Despite the efforts of some OSU faculty and staff to recognize and address the needs of African American female students, these women must still face the ultimate negotiation, communicating effectively without assistance from enough advocates, role models, and mentors.

OSU can boast about its distinguished history of affirmative action initiatives. Praise for OSU is in order in comparison to the lack of commitment and funding initiatives at most large educational institutions; nonetheless, OSU's efforts are woefully inadequate. There is a critical need to employ and maintain African American female faculty and staff to assist their white colleagues in developing an academic and social environment conducive to the success of all students, including African American females.

To date, even though African American women have made up a very large part of minority students entering OSU, no official statistics were available in the Office of Academic Affairs for the exact number of African American staff and faculty who were employed at OSU to assist in meeting these students' needs. To my knowledge, only two African American women hold full professorship in a body of approximately 3,500 full-time faculty. There are no African American women in upper-level management with decision-making capacities in either the Office of Academic Affairs or the Office of the President.

An extracurricular group like Spirit Drama Society was the means I devised to provide at least a listening mechanism for some of these individuals. The more I listened to their needs, the more I knew my primary function was to keep listening with as little criticism as possible. I satisfied my professional and personal commitments as faculty advisor to Spirit by developing a number of sensory techniques to help them read nonverbal communication patterns more effectively.

Through sensory, Spirit and other techniques students learned the primary role that fear plays in daily communications. Since African American women today are four times more likely than white women to be subjected to physical violence on and off campus, I was committed to developing ways for these female students to be prepared for trouble before it arrived. Through sensory techniques, I taught African American females (and males) to see, hear, smell, taste, and touch elements of fear in themselves and other people. Both Spirit Drama Society's formal performance training and special communications workshops empowered students to translate their dreams into realities as they daily negotiated OSU's labyrinth with increased confidence and determination.

THREE ROLE MODELS WHOSE ACTIONS SPEAK LOUDER THAN WORDS

The first example of a role model whose actions speak louder than words is an African American female OSU alumna who successfully negotiated social and political environments in higher education, Dr. Evelyn Luckey. Dr. Luckey is a former Assistant Superintendent of the Columbus Public Schools. At one point in her distinguished career, she took on the awesome responsibilities of Acting Superintendent. She did all the work, but she didn't get the title. When asked if that is part of the communication challenges for African American women in education, she responded by saying, "I really think so. Because it's very hard for some people to see women taking certain roles." She indicated the means that she has used during her career to overcome communication challenges:

Well, I think I've used a number of things, and I think that's because of the age that I am and when I grew up. I'm very clear about what it is I want to do and want to say. However, there are many ways that you go at these things. And I'm not always confrontational about it. There are other ways.

One of the ways that I've worked is to listen to people; let them talk to me. I think that's part of communication, because what it enables you to do is to build that rapport, that link, that I think is so important. You also begin to see the basis of what it is you want to say to them, because you see where they're coming from. I've read a lot about this since then, but I think I've just learned about this growing up.

I grew up in a very strong household. My mother is a very strong person, a very quiet person. She comes from a family of very strong women, and I had the privilege to know some of them.

I think you sort of learn without knowing you're learning it. What may seem to be different sometimes is not really different. It's building a relationship that enables you to keep on doing what it is you do.

There are many angles to communication. I think that probably one of the things that I have found important to recognize and understand is that what you hear—or what you see—isn't necessarily what is happening. In your communicating, you have to do the same thing, in a sense, in reverse.

A second role model whose actions speak louder than words is Dr. Sekai Holland. Her work has international implications. She is Professor in Communications at the University of Zimbabwe, Southern Africa, and a frequent lecturer in universities throughout the United States. She was a co-convener of the International Black Women's Cross Cultural Summer Institute in New York City in 1988. I interviewed Dr. Holland as a resource person for "African American History Re-told," a ten-part radio docudrama series. Dr. Holland offers these comments in support of African American women in the linkage of the African diaspora:

Both my parents were teachers. My mother started her own school for her own people; she came from a very poor background and when she finished she was offered a scholarship to take a degree in South Africa. She had gotten her education by washing bedsheets in a hospital. In learning at school, she became tops.

She didn't have shoes to wear to the graduation and the missionaries lent her shoes for the night. She went back to her people and built a school; she left the school to become a wife to my father and a mother to me. When she resumed her career, she was a teacher and a broadcaster. She was in the news media for development.

And my daddy was a teacher and a newspaperman. He was a member of Parliament in the federal government and after that he went to the United States in '56 and met people like Dr. Martin Luther King, Jr., Nat King Cole, and Fats Domino. I remember all the photographs and Marian Anderson's book, *Oh Lord, What a Morning*. I was raised on that kind of thinking. I was encouraged to go to Tuskegee University, because that is where I would get the best education. Booker T. Washington's *Up from Slavery* was our Bible. So that is the kind of background that our parents had. They tried to drum into us the link [of the diaspora]. That is when I was still at primary school or elementary school, as you call it, listening to all of these stories from my father when he came from the United States.

Why I'm explaining these things is that there are those Africans in the United States, and on the continent of Africa, who have always been aware of the link and the importance of raising [all the black children of the diaspora] to be aware of the link. These Africans insisted the children accept the responsibility that they have to make the connection with the other people who were lost to America or have been thrown out of Africa. [Our collective] experience would actually help to form the foundation for a better life, not just for the African children or the African women, but for the African diaspora as a whole.

That is where we differ with the other [white] women. We see the basis for the struggle as lying in ourselves as black women, defining our own reality for ourselves, as a way of throwing light on how we can survive.

Dr. Maya Angelou is the third role model whose actions speak louder than words. She is an award-winning author, distinguished performer, and profound lecturer. She is the ultimate communicator for African American women who insist upon getting the best for themselves through lives of service. In a series of autobiographical works, she has courageously outlined her success and failures at communicating or being heard as an African American female in numerous hostile environments. She shared the following thoughts in my interview with her in the 1970s:

I want to become a great poet. And I don't mean just write great poetry but to live a poetic existence. What I mean by that is to take responsibility for the time I'm taking up and the space I occupy.

There was a statement made by Terence, the Roman playwright, 150 B.C. The statement is that "I am a human being. Nothing human can be alien to me." It is interesting that the man's name is Terentius Afer, or Terence of Africa. He was a slave. Sold to a Roman senator. Freed by the Roman senator. He became Rome's most important playwright. Six plays are here in your university's library, by Terence. And that statement, "I am a human being; therefore, nothing human can be alien to me."

Now I internalized that many, many years ago. I didn't know that he was an African. I just believed that. What I want to grow to is to understand that. That's what I am about. That's what I think is a poetic existence. When one agrees with John Donne, you don't ask "For whom the bell tolls." It tolls for you, every time. And the loss of life of every human being diminishes me. I want to really understand that. I want to be that. That's my dream. To be a great human being.

As a writer, communicator, and advocate of "quality living," I challenge all fellow educators to join Dr. Maya Angelou in striving to be great human beings. Although this means putting a part of ourselves aside in the interest of the common good, being great human beings does not mean abandoning or neglecting ourselves or our personal goals. It means using our time, talent, and resources to enhance the quality of living for all others.

The ultimate negotiation for African American women and their colleagues in higher education must be to develop communication among fellow educators. These educators must teach and learn well, whether they are "credentialed" university professors or wise souls with invaluable knowledge to share. We must sustain and strengthen our courage to experiment and grow personally and professionally. Only then can we willingly acknowledge others' needs without fear of failing them or ourselves. When we reach these goals, we will experience moments of greatness as human beings, adventurous communicators who have successfully negotiated the ultimate challenge—facing ourselves fearlessly. Then we can continue to develop the well-educated, balanced world citizens that the present and future demand.

6

The Emergence of Black Women as College Presidents

M. Colleen Jones

In the United States in 1990 there are twenty-five collegiate chief executive officers who are Black women (Jones 1991). To put that number into perspective, there are approximately 3,000 colleges and universities, and 296 of them have women presidents (Office of Women in Higher Education 1988). A comprehensive search of the literature reveals that very few studies have been conducted that focused exclusively on women college presidents. Generally, these women chief executives are included in broader studies of college presidents, but since women only represent about 10% of the population of college presidents, their comparatively small numbers within these samples mitigate against any insightful or meaningful analysis. Those studies that have concentrated on women presidents centered on general demographic information and patterns and personal career histories. No study has focused on the developmental experiences and personalities of women college presidents by looking to their backgrounds to determine the antecedent factors that cultivated the skills, talents, and abilities they bring to and utilize in their daily activities. My research, which has the working title An Exploratory and Descriptive Study of the Cognitive Attributes, Life Experiences, and Leadership Styles of Black Women College Presidents, will examine various factors associated with leadership skill and leadership style development among Black women college presidents. The intent of the study is to determine whether these women have similar personalities and comparable leadership-developing activities and life experiences, and how those factors influenced their present leadership style.

Not unlike the European schools after which those in America were designed, collegiate education in the colonies was reserved for men. Without belaboring the sociological and historical precedents for the exclusion of women, it is significant that in spite of those barriers, in the early 1800s female academies and seminaries were established (even though primarily as "finishing schools" for "proper ladies"). The first women's college was established in 1836 in Macon, Georgia (the Wesleyan Female College), with most of the growth in the collegiate education of women occurring after the first Morrill Act (passed in 1862, also known as the "Land-Grant College Act") and the Civil War (Brubaker and Rudy 1976). Little is known about the genesis or leadership of many of these institutions. Sophia Smith is believed to be the first woman to establish and lead a college (Smith College, established in 1875), and she was unique in that regard (Brubaker and Rudy 1976). The first woman president of a college for women (founded by someone else) was Alice Freeman Palmer in 1880; and the first woman to head a coeducation institution was Dr. Mary L. Gambrell in 1898 (Phagan 1982). While the liberals and feminists of the late 1800s were successful in expanding educational opportunities for girls and women, the leadership of those institutions remained the domain of men well into the twentieth century.

If women administrators in colleges and universities were practically neglected in research, Black women in collegiate administration weren't even acknowledged. Even in the historically Black colleges there are virtually no chronicles of the few women who held positions of authority. Noteworthy is the fact that the earliest of the Black women chief administrators (e.g., Mary McLeod Bethune, Mattie Cook, and others) were women who founded the institutions they led (Giddings 1984; Chase 1987). Over the last twenty-five years, fewer than forty Black women have persisted through the arduous search process to be appointed chief executive of a college or university. In 1990, there are twenty-five Black women college presidents; 36% of them have been appointed since 1987 (Jones 1991).

My study, which has been underwritten by an American Fellowship from the American Association of University Women, explores the realm of Black women who are college presidents. It will present descriptive information about their personalities and leadership styles that will provide a basis for subsequent research. A recent study discussed demographic characteristics (age, family history, education, and so forth) of twelve of these women (Chase 1987) and analyzed their perceptions of the major job roles, problems, expectations, and experiences of being "the president." The Chase study stands alone in its focus on Black women. Other studies (McGee 1978; Willie 1976; Cole 1984; Fobbs 1988) have examined either women in administrative roles or the (male) presidents of Black colleges.

The consequence of being both Black and female, as well as president, is a novel construct for researchers. Searches of four major literature databases (Management Abstracts; Educational Resources Information Clearinghouse (ERIC); Center for Research on Women; and Dissertation Abstracts, International) spanning the last fifteen years have located about fifty major empirical or meta-analytical articles, theses, research studies, or speeches about Black women in collegiate leadership positions (department chair, up). My study seeks to fill that abyss by exploring and describing the leadership styles, life experiences, and personality types of Black women college presidents.

What do we know so far about these exemplary women? From data I have compiled we know the following: As noted earlier, there are twenty-five Black women chief executive officers in academe. Contrary to their Black male counterparts, the majority of Black women presidents head non-Black institutions (18:25). Slightly over half are located at community colleges; another fourth are at B.A.-granting institutions; and the remainder are located at master's/doctoral level universities. These institutions are located across the United States, almost equally distributed between Midwestern, Northeastern, Southern, and Western sectors. Three-fourths of the institutions are state or locally controlled; two are independent; and four others are church-sponsored. Two of the institutions are women's colleges.

On a more personal level (Chase 1987), the mean age is fifty-one years old, with the age at presidential appointment being forty-five. Three-fourths were not married at the time of their appointment (never married, widowed, or divorced) and most have children, many of whom are of high school age or older. While not all of the women have doctorates, the majority of those who do hold Ph.D.s—and their fields range from educational administration to the natural sciences to Greek literature.

This is a very interesting and diverse group of women, who individually and collectively have a record of professional achievement as well as a strong commitment to education. These are common components that stimulated their attainment of the pinnacle of educational leadership, a college presidency. My research seeks to assemble a fuller, multidimensional model of who these women are and what factors may have contributed to their ascendance to college presidencies. But at its essence, this is a study of leadership development and the manifestation of "leader qualities" in an identifiable leadership "style."

The context for this research is the premise that the kind of person you are (i.e, your cognitive style or attributes), in tandem with the opportunities, experiences, and models you have had, defines your capacity for leadership and influences your leadership style. Our society, educational institutions, and role expectations have more readily encouraged and provided leadership opportunities for male children than for female children. Many of the Black women college presidents were born before 1945, so they grew up in a era when girls' opportunities were narrowly framed. Although they also experienced the collateral bond of racism, somehow these women effectively extracted the positive from their environment. They then utilized it to project themselves to truly unique positions of accomplishment and authority.

Because Black women in leadership positions in higher education represent an emerging cohort, I decided to utilize widely recognized leadership and cognitive style assessment instruments, so that this study would offer baseline data that would facilitate future comparative studies with other populations. The Myers-Briggs Type Indicator (MBTI) (Myers and Briggs 1977) will be used to define the cognitive attributes of the Black women college presidents. The MBTI will also indicate if a "residential" profile exists, or if the Black women college presidents follow the personality type patterns of other college-educated women; educational administrators, corporate managers, or teacher-educators. The Multifactor Leadership Questionnaire (MLQ) (Bass 1985) will categorize the individual study participants, leadership style being more or less transactional or transformational (Burns 1978; Bass 1985). There is no valuative intent associated with the use of these instruments; no claims about a "better" leadership style or an optimum set of cognitive attributes will be made. The aim is to explore the realm of a virtually unstudied population in order to provide data that will stimulate future research, and to raise the level of inquiry beyond the "distinctly personal" to that of a class of individuals. Rather than to reinforce the exemplary nature of these women's achievements and exploit their uniqueness by utilizing a purely case study approach, this study will strive to determine the existence of patterns and relationships among the cognitive attributes, leadership-developing activities, and life experiences of Black women who have become college presidents.

Toward that end, this study employs the following working hypotheses:

Cognitive Style/Personality

• The cognitive attributes profiles of the Black women presidents will not generally resemble those of corporate executives or other high-level academic administrators.

Life Experiences

• Role models and mentors (male and female) had attributable influence in the formation of an approach to leadership.
• There is a parallel pattern of life experiences among the Black women college presidents.

Leadership-Developing Activities

• There is a similar chronicle of leadership-developing activities that preceded these women's decisions to seek a college presidency.
• There are specific experiences and challenges that Black women college presidents recognize as being essential to the acquisition of skills necessary to be a college president.

Leadership Style

• Black women presidents will perceive themselves and be identified (by working colleagues, peers, and associates) as being more transformational than transactional in their leadership style.
• Black women college presidents will see their leadership philosophy and style as being the result of conscious decisions and purposeful objectives throughout their lives.

This study gains its significance from the dearth of information available on Black professionals (in general); Black collegiate administrators; and, more specifically, Black women executives in academe. Most of the articles, treatises, and commentaries about Blacks concentrate on racial deficits and pathologies. There are a few studies and reviews of fully functioning, "average" go-to-work-every-day Black people; there are almost none on high achieving, above-the-curve, middle-class Black people. It seemed as if most of the research was conducted with the purpose of fortifying the negative stereotypes and with no desire to examine Black people, and especially Black women administrators, to determine if their presence was a serendipitous occurrence or just simply not studied by previous researchers. A consequent and personal motivation for pursuing this research was to look at those who W. E. B. DuBois called "the talented tenth" and to set forth a paradigm that would highlight the good, strong, positive, and right that has evolved and will continue to emerge from the Black community.

In the management literature, studies of women in professional positions first began to appear during the 1970s. These studies gained richness from the variety of disciplines and working environments examined, and they have greatly contributed to interdisciplinary research. Some of the more notable pieces of work in the management, leadership, and psychology literature have been produced by women. *The Managerial Woman* (Henning and Jardim 1976); *Men and Women of the Corporation* (Kanter 1977); *Paths to Power* (Josefowitz 1980); *The Androgynous Manager* (Sargent 1981); *Women and Men as Leaders* (Heller 1982); *In a Different Voice* (Gilligan 1982); and *Feminine Leadership* (Loden 1985) all have left a mark on the way women are perceived in organizations, as well as the way women perceive themselves as they pursue "the road less traveled."

These works are not without their staunch critics. Nevertheless, we cannot shy away from doing research and disseminating it because of the rigors and vagaries of scrutiny—regardless of how appropriate or petty it may be. The irony, however, is that while many of those studies were done by faculty or research fellows in colleges and universities, their work rarely focused on the academy. Within academe many changes were occurring, not the least important of which was the expanding numbers of women in positions of authority and leadership. It is alarming that there are so few studies that provide any insight for how these women came to be who they are. The underlying premise, therefore, postulates that the development of leadership acumen and the acquisition of leadership skills is a likely outcome for women who have similar cognitive attributes and comparable leadership-developing activities and life experiences. Data for this research were being collected while this book was being assembled. An abstract of the findings as well as the complete dissertation is available from me. The process of developing the conceptual model for the research, as well as spending seemingly endless hours trying to find the empirical antecedents for research of this nature, has afforded me some wisdom that I will share with you.

As I have addressed a variety of audiences about women in corporate and academic leadership positions, the receptions have varied from politely condescending to lukewarm to genuinely excited. The logic that permeates many editorial boards, grant proposal review and doctoral committees, and tenure review panels is that if it's not about men, preferably white men, then it's not worth doing—that is, it has no relevance or significance. Fortunately, that is a diminishing perspective, but it does not facilitate the work or soothe the battle scars of those of us who "toil in the vineyard" of academic research about women and people of color. There are issues of control, power, access, and so forth that too often figure into the equation of what constitutes "scholarly research" or "relevant inquiry." Nevertheless, those apparent stumbling blocks must be used as stepping stones, and we must be more assertive in our efforts to promote diversity in research and throughout academe.

It is imperative that with resolve, energy, creativity, and persistence we continue to conduct our own research on women and people of color, and to encourage and assist the efforts of others. In the process, we need to be committed to diversity in our teaching materials and strategies; be more supportive and utilize interdisciplinary approaches to research and andragogy; and seek opportunities to insure that our "different voice" is heard.

During the 1980s Black women emerged throughout the administrative ranks of higher education (Moses 1989). That there are now twenty-five who serve as presidents of colleges or universities is an indication of the dramatic shifts that are slowly but significantly changing the nature and face of academe. These women did not just appear—their appointment represented a culmination and recognition of years of accomplishments. My research seeks to illuminate the personal and experiential factors that were significant to their development of leadership acumen and the evolution of their leadership style. Most studies of college and university presidents focus on examinations of presidential choices during times of campus or personal stress, career paths to the presidency, or historical case studies of former chief executives. Rarely have we been given insights into the noncurricular, extraprofessional aspects that made the person presidential (i.e., a leader). It is that kind of examination of the cognitive attributes and leadership-developing activities of a unique subset (Black women) of a select population (women) of college and university presidents that distinguishes my research from that which is generally found in the literature. It should also stimulate similar inquiries of other emerging cohorts in a variety of disciplines.

III

Hispanic Women and Higher Education

In this section the roles and dilemmas of Hispanic women in higher education are explored. Sarah Nieves-Squires emphasizes the need for sensitivity to cultural differences, and suggests that we should celebrate the diversity rather than trying to avoid it. In her chapter, she identifies some of the barriers which have inhibited the recruitment and retention of Hispanic women in institutions of higher education.

Anita Leal and Cecilia Menjivar studied intra-ethnic differences among Hispanic women in higher education. They found that there was little mutual support given by Hispanic women who came from different countries to each other. They also found that the Hispanic women studied did not network or mentor each other.

7

Hispanic Women in the U.S. Academic Context

Sarah Nieves-Squires

The social climate for Hispanas in academia is fraught with many barriers. Some of the most disturbing ones are encountered in the realm of collegial social intercourse. Ignorance of mores and folkways usually prompts non-Hispanics to misunderstand social cues such as expressions of congeniality. Unfortunately, a lot of the information stored in the collective imagination about different segments of the Hispanic population rests on Broadway's *West Side Story* for imagery about the Puerto Ricans and Hollywood's *El Norte* and *La Bamba* for interpretations of the Central and Mexican American ethos, respectively. Even then, this perception is true only for the most aware. For most, the differences are not even perceived. Thus, a warm smile is mistaken for a flirtatious one; expansive gesticulation is interpreted as lack of verbal ability; closer personal space is perceived as a sign of inviting intimacy. The problem is compounded for the Hispana who has chosen to retain most of the social values prevalent among her cultural group, because this persistence is regarded as deviant, if not totally wanton, behavior by fellow academics. On the other hand, members of her own community are often prone to refer with contempt to the "coconuts" in their midst.

This chapter will examine some of the issues and conditions that female Hispanic Americans face when they participate in the higher education establishment in the United States. It is hoped that the chapter will contribute to the rethinking of priorities and projections for the future participation of Hispanic Americans as full-fledged partners in the intellectual, social, and economic growth of the country.

The chapter is divided into six sections: (1) Introduction; (2) Current Status of Women in Academia; (3) How the Experience of Hispanas Differs; (4) Socioeconomic Climate; (5) Issues of Import; and (6) Recommendations. In the introduction, attention is drawn to the diversity of the Hispanic population at large in the United States, highlighting its level of educational attainment and how it has an impact on the way Hispanas experience academia. The second section gives an overview of the status of women in general in academia, both as students (graduate and undergraduate) and as faculty members. The discussion includes the issue of unequal remuneration. Section three considers the way in which the experience of Hispanas differs from that of women in general, at the levels of degree acquisition and induction into faculty and administrative ranks. Section four explores the socioeconomic climate that undergirds the academic system and leads to a discussion of issues that I deem important when considering the academic climate as experienced by Hispanas. The issues of import examined in section five are:

• The explanations proffered by academia regarding the status of Hispanas in their midst
• Social barriers encountered by Hispanas in academia
• Standards for judging credentials and performance of Hispanas in academia
• Affirmative Action policies
• Class distinctions and cultural isolation

Section six explores how the black Hispanas experience academia, and section seven offers recommendations.

One of the motivations behind this exploration is the recognition that as the population growth rate of the United States has been experiencing an overall downward trend over the past twenty years, minority groups are manifesting a growth rate two to fourteen times greater than those experienced by the nonminority population. This higher growth rate reflects the youthfulness (having more members of childbearing age) more than the higher rate of fertility exhibited by minority populations. In the case of the Hispanic American population, its ranks have been consistently growing at a rate that is about twice as high as that of the nonminority population. But population trends among the Hispanic population in the United States are not solely linked to soaring birth rates. They are greatly influenced by immigration also, which in turn responds to the prevailing economy in this country and its impact on the neighboring economies of Mexico, South and Central America, and the Caribbean Basin.

For some time now, the U.S. population has been alerted to the demographic reversal that is taking place—data project that a state such as California will become a "minority" majority state by the year 2000. Thus, as we career toward the next century, it behooves us to take a closer look at one of those groups from which the "person power" to sustain the economy of this country in the year 2000 and beyond will emerge.

INTRODUCTION

Although it is not generally acknowledged, the Hispanic population of this country is far from monolithic. In the Southeast, the Cubans lead in numbers as well as in influence; in the Northeast, the Puerto Ricans outnumber other Spanish-speaking groups; in the Midwest and the Southwest, the Chicanos prevail. The Mid-Atlantic Hispanic population is generously sprinkled with other Caribbean islanders, as well as with Central and South American refugees who are received by previous émigrés, who themselves are scattered around the larger cities and urban centers of the country but are found in larger enclaves in the New York–Washington corridor. This is worth noting because the status and provenance of the various Spanish-speaking groups are tied to their expectations of what their experience in this country should be and to the adaptations they are willing to undergo in order to survive. Class distinctions and cultural isolation do not necessarily haunt all members of this heterogeneous group to the same extent, although it can be argued that the haunting is there for all to experience to lesser or greater extent.

Educational Attainment

Census statistics in 1987 showed that 8.5% of all Hispanics over the age of twenty-five were college graduates, as opposed to 20.6% of the same age cohort among the non-Hispanic population in the United States. In 1986 the total Hispanic enrollment in public and private institutions of higher education amounted to 624,000, of those 292,000 were men, and 332,000 were women. While the absolute numbers of Hispanic college students is increasing, the gains are not keeping pace with population increases. According to the Bureau of the Census, the number of Hispanic Americans aged nineteen to twenty-four (the age group where college students are concentrated) grew by 62% (from 1,551,000 in 1976 to 2,513,000 in 1986) over the last decade. The number of Hispanic Americans in that age group enrolled in college during that same period increased only by 43% (from 309,000 to 433,000), which amounts to 5% of the total enrollment at all institutions of higher education. This represents an increase when compared with a representation of 3.5% in 1976. Of all Hispanics in colleges, 43% are enrolled in community colleges rather than in four-year institutions (Center for Education Statistics 1988).

Diversity

Due to the diversity of the Hispanic population and its varying degrees of participation in mainstream U.S. society, the educational attainment varies considerably among the various groups. Among Cubans, who comprise 5% of the U.S. Hispanic population, 61.6% had completed at least four years of high school in 1987 and 17.1% had completed four or more years of college. Among Central and South Americans, who constitute 11% of the Hispanic population, 59.3% had finished four years of high school in 1987 and 12.2% had finished four or more years of college. Among Puerto Ricans, who constitute 12% of the total Hispanic population, 53.8% had completed high school but only 8% had finished four or more years of college in 1987. For Mexican Americans, the picture is grimmest: Although they represent 63% of the Hispanics in the land, in 1987 only 44.8% had finished high school and just 5.8% had finished four or more years of college (Fields 1988). The remaining 9% is composed mostly of Spaniards who, like most of the Central and South Americans who traditionally migrated to the United States, are from affluent families and do not partake of the minority culture. Examination of the underlying reasons for the disparity in numbers offers one of the keys to better understanding the status and diversity of the Hispanic American population in the United States. The most substantive explanation resides in the demographics of the various subgroups that are known collectively as Hispanic Americans.

The Cuban Population

Those who arrived in this country in great numbers as refugees and with the blessing of the State Department in the 1960s form the core of the Cuban Americans. It is an older population characterized by high levels of educational attainment and light complexions. There is a second tier of Cuban migration, those who arrived in the mid-1980s as a result of the Mariel boatlift. They have not fared as well. They are darker in complexion, have lower levels of educational attainment and socioeconomic status, and had less official help toward assimilation into the U.S. mainstream than earlier refugees.

Central and South Americans

Traditionally, it has been the upper-class persons who have come to the United States to further their education or establish business contacts. They mostly identify themselves as Latin Americans and enjoy a comfortable standard of living. The most recent arrivals, however, may be escaping various forms of repression and hoping to "establish themselves in an advantageous position to be able to help loved ones still living and struggling in the old country" (Stanford News 1988). They do not enjoy the same privileged standard of living as the earlier arrivals.

Puerto Ricans

Although it is unknown to some, Puerto Ricans are no more immigrants than the Blacks who move from the South to the industrial North, since they are born U.S. citizens by virtue of the Foraker Act, which granted U.S. citizenship to all Puerto Ricans born in Puerto Rico or in the United States as of 1917. They are at the core of the Hispanic Caribbean Basin migration, which includes Dominicans and Cubans. The latter, however, do not partake of the U.S. citizenship. Puerto Ricans frequently travel between their mainland and the United States. It is an essentially young, urbanized population.

Mexican Americans

They were a presence in the Southwest even before the Mayflower arrived but have been placed in a minority status in this country since the annexation of some of their land to the United States. Their numbers are swelled by Mexican nationals who cross the border in order to better their economic condition. This segment of the population grew by 93% between 1970 and 1980, according to the Center for Education Statistics (CFES) (1988). Their educational level is the lowest among the Hispanics, which may be due in part to the high proportion of agricultural workers in their midst.

One of the factors that has slowed the progress of Hispanic Americans in higher education is the absence of Hispanic counterparts to the historically Black colleges such as Tuskegee Institute or Morehouse College. The one exception is Boricua College, which was established as a Puerto Rican institution and serves 1,000 students at three sites in Brooklyn and Manhattan. Another crucial factor is financial, which influences the choice and pursuit of education for Hispanic students at a higher rate than the general population. This financial influence is understandable, given that in 1986 24.7% of all Hispanic families lived below the poverty level, as compared to 9% of all families in the country. Thus, the Hispanic students are more likely to go to college where they can get financial aid, rather than where they can attain the education to which they aspire.

The Experience of Hispanas

Female participation in the education sphere has proved to be the area in which Hispanic women have had an edge on adaptation strategies over Hispanic men in this country. While the reasons for this phenomenon are arguable, the fact remains that Hispanic women outstrip Hispanic men in educational attainment. This is not the case when the numbers include all persons of Spanish-speaking origin and include those who (although they are Spanish speakers) come from backgrounds that are not perceived as minorities and who identify themselves not as Hispanics but as Latin Americans. While the identification of Latin American versus Hispanic may vary according to geographic location, generally, "Latin American" refers to Spanish speakers who do not share hyphenated citizenship and whose class and socioeconomic interests are associated with minorities. This is a particularly sensitive issue in academia, where for affirmative action purposes both kinds of Spanish speakers are included in Hispanic minority counts.

CURRENT STATUS OF WOMEN IN ACADEMIA

In order to place the status of Hispanas in academia in proper perspective, one must consider it within the more generalized framework of women in academia. Although there has been an increase in the number and percentage of women students, the status of women in academia in the late 1980s had not changed radically, in absolute terms, from their status twenty years ago. This is true at all levels of the academic experience. The following profiles of females in the various ranks bear this testimony.

Graduate and Undergraduate Students

In 1981 women made up more than half of the undergraduate and graduate student population. However, data from the Center for Education Statistics show that as we progressed up the academic ladder, women made up less than one-quarter of the professional students and received only 31.5% of all doctorates. Nevertheless, these figures represent a 27% increase at the bachelor's degree level, an 800% increase in first professional degrees, and a 100% increase in doctorates during the period 1970–1980. For the period 1976–1986, the distribution of enrollment between men and women has reversed itself; in 1976, 53% of those enrolled were men and 47% women. In 1986, 47% of those enrolled were men and 53% women. Fall enrollment in all institutions in 1986 showed 4,000,133 women out of a total enrollment of 12,500,700 (CFES 1988).

Faculty Members

Even though women have been making up a larger percentage of those currently being hired to faculty positions (in 1980, 22.4% of the newly hired in universities were women, as compared to 14.7% in 1972; in four-year colleges, 28% of those hired in 1980 were women, as opposed to 19% in 1972), the gap is nowhere near to being closed. In 1987, women held only 27.5% of all faculty positions (CFES 1988). While there has been an increase in the hiring of women in academia, the increase has been particularly sharp in areas where women have been in the minority, that is, in fields such as mathematics, physics/astronomy, chemistry, earth sciences, and engineering. A disproportionate number of women are serving in part-time positions or as lecturers and instructors, positions that are off the tenure track and lack the possibility of promotion. Women also continue to hold a higher share of positions outside their primary sphere of interest and are still more likely to be found in lower status institutions, such as teacher-training and two-year colleges. Women faculty are also more likely to be found at women's colleges rather than coed ones, at smaller institutions than larger ones, and are less likely to be at prestigious, research-oriented universities. For Ph.D. holders in science, more women than men are employed part-time, in nonscience jobs. Women still hold 44% of the full-time, non–tenure track positions, but only 18% of the full, associate, or assistant professorships. In 1988, women still tend to be clustered at the lower end of the academic ladder. Being clustered at the lower end of the academic ladder is more likely to be true in prestigious institutions, and it is as true today as it was twenty-five years ago.

Remuneration

In academic year 1982–1983, female assistant and associate professors earned 94% of the salary earned by men. Overall, women's salaries in academia were 83% of males' salaries. In addition, the longer women have been employed, the smaller their salary is likely to be in relation to mens'. The average salaries for men and women faculty in 1983–1984 show that the gap still exists even though there have been recent efforts to equalize salaries by giving women equal or greater salary increases. In the humanities, where women have received 7.7% salary increases compared to 6% for men, their average salaries are still almost $4,500

less. At public institutions, with a 5% larger increase, women's salaries
still lag $5,000 behind. According to Angela Simeone,

these data demonstrate the cumulative effects of discrimination, as discrimination against women early in their careers is perpetuated and magnified as
their careers progress. The percentage of increase for men and women at different ranks for different institutional types is fairly similar, with men having a
small advantage in most categories. However, because salary increases begin
from a base salary, the gap widens as a lower starting salary is compounded by
lower annual increments. (Simeone 1986)

However, according to Simeone, there is evidence that women may be
more likely today than in the past to receive equal compensation for
equal performance.

HOW THE EXPERIENCE OF HISPANAS DIFFERS

Within that general scenario, the presence of Hispanas is even more
tenuous. In the most recent past, we can point to the institutionalization
of bilingual education across the country as being largely instrumental
in the opening of access for Hispanas to positions in education in general
and, to a smaller degree, to positions in higher education. To this day,
however, the degree of invisibility of Hispanas in higher education remains painfully high. One of the explanations that is offered to account
for the level of attainment of Hispanas in higher education rests within
the framework of the general educational attainment of the Hispanic
population of the United States. However, in 1986 there were 145,775
Hispanas enrolled in all institutions of higher education, or 23% of the
total Hispanic enrollment. Of those, 53% were enrolled in four-year
colleges. They also constituted 54% of the Hispanic enrollment in two-
year institutions (CFES 1988). Compare this with 1976, when only 5.9%
of Mexican American women and 3.8% of Puerto Rican women had
completed four or more years of college.

Hispanic enrollment has risen steadily since 1976, breaking the 6 million mark in 1986. In 1985, Hispanic women earned 2.7% of the master's
degrees awarded and 2.2% of the doctoral degrees. The participation
rates in college enrollment of Hispanics between the ages of twenty-five
and thirty-four have consistently exceeded those of Whites in that same
age bracket for the past ten years (CFES 1988). These data would support
the thesis that lack of opportunity is probably more of an explanation
than lack of interest for the paucity in representation.

Faculty Members

According to the latest Office for Civil Rights figures, Hispanics constitute 1.5% of all faculty and just 1.1% of all tenured faculty. These

numbers include all fields of the professorate and report all Hispanics including the previously mentioned Latin Americans (persons from Spain, Brazil, Portugal, and South America who are routinely identified as "minority" Hispanic faculty) (CFES 1988). M. Olivas also reports "startling evidence that minority faculty were not even reasonably represented in the least prestigious sector—community colleges—where few faculty hold the doctorate or engage in research" (1988). According to Olivas, although the number of women in faculty positions has probably increased as a result of Affirmative Action programs, there are still very few Spanish-speaking women in high-level academic positions, in spite of the fact that in terms of actual enrollment numbers Hispanic women outnumber Hispanic men. Hispanic men exceed the number of Hispanic women employed as instructional and administrative staff. As a respondent to my questionnaire pointed out in the Arts and Sciences, "Hispanic men are employed in Romance Languages and are able to be recognized more openly."

Top Administrative Positions

After twenty years of Affirmative Action, the appointment of Hispanics to chief executive positions remains rare. California and Texas are two of the most populous states in the union and are home to the largest Hispanic populations in the nation. Both have a high number of postsecondary institutions with the greatest number of Hispanics in attendance. They also have the greatest number of Hispanics as faculty. Yet in the University of California system, which has 9 chancellors and 27 vice-chancellors, there are no Hispanic chancellors or vice-chancellors. In the California State University system, which has 16 campus presidents and 30 vice-presidents, only one president is Hispanic. There are no Hispanics at the vice-president level. In the University of Texas system, there are no Hispanics among the 7 campus presidents. Out of 10 vice-presidents there is just one Hispanic vice-president. The three systems in the two states provide a total of 108 executive positions and show only 2 Hispanic appointments (Valverde 1988). Of those, none are female. Unfortunately, even in those cases where a Hispana is appointed to a high-level administrative position, acknowledgement and equal treatment are begrudged.

SOCIOECONOMIC CLIMATE

The experience of Hispanas in academia is not unique. The total number of minority women employed as full-time faculty in 1976 amounted to 3%. The breakdown by ethnic groups told a disheartening story: Of all minority women employed in 1976, 0.4% were Hispanas; 2% were

Black; 0.4% Asian; and less than 0.1% were Native American (CFES 1988). The situation has not greatly improved in the intervening years, even though there has been an increase in the numbers of minority women who receive higher education degrees and who are eager to enter the academic ranks. As mentioned before, the underrepresentation of women in academia is not limited to minorities. However, the situation is worse for Hispanas than for White females because of their unequal starting point. It would appear that the pattern of women's exclusion from better-paying jobs is more pervasive than exclusion on account of race, as Ivan Illich points out (1982). When the dimension of race is added to the exclusion by gender, however, the odds are unevenly stacked against minority women. Ironically, the education process provides one of the best examples of routine discrimination against women worldwide. Even when (as mentioned by Illich) in different countries the educational process for both men and women is of equal length, even if the curricula to which both sexes are exposed are the same, the consistent result everywhere is a lower lifetime salary for women than for men. Indeed, according to Illich, the more advanced the levels of education scaled, the more tightly are women locked into their place, for they then have less chance than men for a new start on a different track. Thus, the plight of the Hispanas in academia has to be examined within this context—the context of socially condoned unequal treatment of females. "The battles of the 1970s may have opened the executive suite to women, but this change has disproportionately benefited sisters from privileged backgrounds" (Illich 1982).

The lack of representation of Hispanas in academia as faculty members cause them to be overburdened by an inordinate amount of student advisees—both those who are formally assigned and those who gravitate toward their doors. There is a tacit assumption that all Hispanic students should be advised by the sole Hispanic faculty member even when the numbers outstrip those assigned to other faculty members. Rather than hiring more Hispanas as faculty, administrators try to solve the problem of isolation and dearth of role models on campus by lumping them all at the sole Hispana's doorstep. The sheer effort of trying to do well by the students while at the same time routing an academic career that encompasses scholarly research, excellent teaching, and committee participation insures that very few Hispanas remain within the academic ranks. It would be easy to dismiss this phenomenon as one of bad faith on the part of those who make these decisions in order to best sabotage the Hispanas on board. However, given the rather meager numbers of Hispanas presently pursuing careers in academia, one wonders why those few who find their way to positions in academia would be perceived as a threat to the status of nonminority women and men who are already ensconced among its ranks. Thus, one has to assume that the underlying reason is lack of understanding of all the elements involved, not purposive negative action. A unique economic aspect related to the presence of Hispanic students on campus is the fact that not all Hispanas enjoy U.S. citizenship. Assuming that all Hispanas on campus either are or are not citizens prima facie places students in a doubly disadvantaged position. If they are citizens, they are rarely apprised of avenues that are available in this country for helping them to subsidize their studies.

ISSUES OF IMPORT

In order to best understand the experience of Hispanas in academia, I thought it useful to look at the realm of acculturation and assimilation that engulfs them—in addition to, rather than uniquely from, a gender/ ethnic-related differential treatment basis. Thus, I will explore the academic climate for Hispanas by questioning the explanations of academics and by casting a glance at the cultural pressures that Hispanas endure. I am indebted to Gayatri Chakravorty Spivac for her analysis of marginality in her book, *In Other Worlds: Essays in Cultural Politics* (1987).

The Academic Explanation

What we find in academia by way of explanation resides on two particular modes of behavior:

1. Explanations take so little notice of the surrounding political and economic determinants that they allow academic institutions to continue to present themselves as nothing but a support system for the equality of opportunity and employment of "qualified" employees, without examining why so few Hispanas ever seem to be "qualified." As Spivac points out, mainstream society offers a false sense of power to the few minorities who "think like us" on the condition that they use it to maintain things as they are. This is the meaning of tokenism—that power withheld from the vast majority of minorities is offered to a few, so that it may appear that any truly qualified minority can gain access to leadership, recognition, and rewards; hence, that justice based on merits actually prevails. The token minority is encouraged to see herself as different from most other members of her group, as exceptionally talented and deserving, and to separate herself from the wider minority condition. At the same time, she is perceived by "ordinary" members of her group as separate also—perhaps even as stronger than themselves. The success of academic tokenism hinges on the marginality of the Hispanic presence in the society at large, which naturally permeates the microworld of academia. After all, it is not the notion of cultural pluralism but the notion of the one over the many that prevails in aca-

demia, embodied in the notions of "merit" and "competence" that reign supreme. Thus, the scenario of tokenism is enacted every time a Hispana is told, "But you don't look Puerto Rican!" (or Hispanic or Latin). What this really means is that you do not conform to the stereotypical idea we hold about members of your collectivity. What this actually communicates is that if indeed one aspires to be one of "Us," one should not insist on highlighting one's differences, doing research on Hispanic topics, speaking in a foreign language with one's co-patriots, or retaining social characteristics that reveal an otherness that the "Us" cannot abide (such as placing a higher premium on collective achievement and eschewing taking credit for individual achievement).

2. In terms of the proliferation of market availability explanations for the dearth of Hispanic representation on campuses, most of the explanations hinge on the imputed unavailability of suitable representatives of the underrepresented groups. What is really being expressed, however, is the dearth of those among the target groups who are like the "Us" in academia. The issue of marginality became central to my exploration of the status of Hispanas in academia. In academia, as well as in the world at large, the putative "center" welcomes selective inhabitants of the margin only to better exclude the margin. Since Hispanas are placed at the periphery, there is no need to consider such issues as the absence of parallelism between population growth and employment levels among Hispanics—either in the U.S. economy at large or in the more restricted economy of academia. As long as the position of Hispanic Americans is one of "permanent marginality" in the economic sphere, academia will continue to treat them as outsiders who are not valued within the academic enterprise. Demographic imperatives may soon require a revised stance. Once again, it is worth noting that the issue of permanent marginality does not apply to Hispanic Americans exclusively but extends to all women in academia, as has been eloquently demonstrated by Angela Simeone in her work on academic women.

Social Barriers Encountered by Hispanas in Academia

For those Hispanas who tread in Anglo and Hispanic worlds, there is an added penalty. The Hispanas' patterns of language and assumptions about self and others and about their collectivity are constantly tested, both by members of their own ethnic group and by professional colleagues. For the former group, she is not "Puertorriquena" or "Chicana" enough, for the latter, she is much too tied to her ethnicity. Too often, the difference in outlook that each of the subgroups of Hispanic Americans bring with them is unrecognized. As I mentioned earlier, the difference in outlook is closely tied to the given group's collective experience in the United States. Thus, for the Puertorriquenas who grow up in Puerto Rico and arrive in this country as young adults to attend institutions of higher education, being called a "spik" does not have the same impact as it does for the "neo-Ricans" who grow up in El Barrio in New York City. "Spik" is a derogatory term used in New York City to denote Hispanics of Puerto Rican origin. It refers to the inability of most Spanish speakers to pronounce a long "i" and short "i" sound differently. "Neo-Rican" refers to Puerto Ricans who are born and/or raised in New York City and thus are more comfortable with New York's inner-city culture. Sometimes it is spelled "New Yorican."

By and large, the incoming Puertorriquena's economic and social background is more likely to be more similar to that of middle-class Anglos than to that of Puerto Ricans born in the inner cities of the United States. In addition, she will have grown up in an atmosphere where she was an integral part of the ethnic "Us," social class and diversity in economic attributes notwithstanding. The impact that this difference implies cannot be overestimated. There is a difference between those growing up among the "Us" that is experienced by those who grow up in Puerto Rico: There is the tension of having to choose a language of communication that may not be their vernacular, when attending primary school. But the difference goes deeper than the level at which either group masters the English language and/or the point at which Spanish is appropriated as a symbol of solidarity. Because unfortunate as it may be, it is a fact that those who grow up in the United States are being singled out as minorities and, thus, as "Them" (Conference Report 1988). The feelings and reactions that such a distinction entails become the norm and in time, though not overtly accepted, are internalized. In many cases, adaptation has meant the rejection of the vernacular for a language that not only does not reflect their cultural heritage but that also might not be shared by most of the significant members of the extended family (thus superimposing an extra layer of conflict to intergenerational relationships and often causing unanticipated rifts). For those who grow up enjoying majority status (as far as any woman can consider herself as such in any culture), the sense of self is in less jeopardy than for those who also have to defend it on ethnic grounds on a daily basis.

Thus, the patterning of cultural differences exhibited by members of these diverse segments of the Spanish-speaking groups are significant and yet are quite unobserved by mainstream Americans in academia. The difference between the perception of Hispanic female students as "retiring and shy" on one hand and the perception of Hispanic faculty members as "proud, aggressive go-getters" on the other lies mostly therein. Because of different cultural assumptions about feminine identification, many Hispanas are unable to gauge how far to go in asserting themselves. Examples of the extremes abound—either too aggressive for comfort, or too shy or retiring. A common reaction is to chastise them for being too aggressive or too shy, a dichotomy that baffles most of those who are unprepared to experience such diversity among the group and/or who have experienced the other set of behaviors and have assumed that they represent the totality of the group's ethos.

Ethnic stereotypes abound, and academia is not immune to them. In addition to the commonly held ones, some academics act under the following assumptions about Hispanas:

1. Thought processes of Hispanas are not as clear as those of Anglos, as betrayed by their hesitation in pursuing oral confrontations, their wide use of gesticulation, and their poor representation in refereed publications.
2. The Hispana's social life is entirely wound up with the Hispanic scene—thus she would be uncomfortable if included in "mainstream" activities.
3. Hispana faculty come from backgrounds so totally different from Anglo faculty that it is not possible or productive to entertain their company in settings other than on campus, if at all.
4. All Hispanas prefer to work with their "own kind," thus it is impractical to place them in departments where there are no Hispanics.
5. Most Hispanas' names are difficult to pronounce, so it is OK to substitute more familiar ones such as "Maria."

Double Standard When Judging Credentials and Performance of Hispanas

One of the more recurrent barriers encountered by Hispanas in academia is the consistent devaluation of their intellectual product—whether it is at the level of research or the relevance of their teaching subject matter. When they are being judged for advancement or retention, the quality of their output is more often than not suspect, particularly if the nature of the research involves themes that are considered minority oriented. If you are Hispanic and do research on themes pertaining specifically to the Hispanic experience, the ensuing work is automatically suspect and carries less weight than the same research conducted by a researcher from a different group. Often, themes of interest to nonmainstream groups are usually shunned by researchers from the mainstream. The rejection or devaluation is usually cloaked under the mantle of lack of "objectivity" and "distancing" from the data. As an Assistant Professor in a large, private research university indicated, "It seems to me that you become a second-class citizen *because* you want to work with your people. There is no recognition that even in your own research you may not be using mainstream's but rather your *own* paradigms." An Associate Dean in a large, private research university explained: "There is a 'deafness' for Hispanic issues—it is as though we are viewed as 'marginal whites.' "

Recurrently, Hispanas attest to the fact that their ideas and/or unfinished product are "appropriated" by mainstream researchers who had convinced them that there was no value in pursuing such avenues of enquiry. As a Program Director in a private research institution commented:

It is still painful for me to evoke my feelings when I was told that a proposal I had written had been adopted and funded, yet there was no mention of my name nor of my crucial contribution in the acknowledged product. At first, I blamed myself and was ashamed and bitter. Then I realized that this had not just happened to me—that this happens to women all the time, and I was just experiencing one more instance of a familiar pattern in the history of women's lives.

Another instance of the double standard for judging credentials and performance of Hispanas resides in the composition of search and review committees. These are the committees on which Hispanas are rarely invited to serve and whose members have the power to determine who will join their ranks and who will remain in their midst. Absence of participation in these committees precludes Hispanas from helping to establish more culturally appropriate ways to assess the accomplishments and promise of members outside the mainstream denomination. A concurrent problem arises from this lack of participation. Whether by lack of understanding of the need for a Hispanic presence or because of fear of being overrun by "them," the members of such committees tend to either (1) raise the standards of induction to such heights that they themselves would not qualify if they were applying for the position, or (2) lower them to such a bare minimum as to insure a predictable inability to cope or survive beyond a semester. Both attitudes evince the same conviction that "they" are not ready to join "our" ranks.

In other instances there is a tendency to forget to mention to the new inductee which areas will count for retention and promotion, when are the best times for participating in certain activities and committees, and when is the best time to propose yourself for advancement and how. This does not always happen out of malice—in many instances, there is simply no social context in which the already inducted interact with the new Hispana inductee.

Given the mandate of the educational enterprise, it is to be expected that talent should not be squandered and that transference of skills should occur between fields. This has not been the case with Hispanas involved in bilingual education programs. The enactment of the Bilingual Education Act was a turning point, a slight opening of the academic door for Hispanic Americans. After a lot of fighting and compromise building, we saw departments of bilingual education spring up in schools of education across the land. While all or most of them were under the aegis of departments of foreign languages and were led by men, at least a crack was opened in the door to academic tenure. It was short-lived. Once the furor for training non Spanish-speaking teachers to teach Spanish-speaking children in the nation's public schools died, the threat of being displaced by "foreign language–speakers" in the local schools was dispelled. The demand for certifiable bilingual teachers waned when some parents started resenting the allocation of funds for the schooling of children whose native tongue was not English. Thus, the training of bilingual teachers went out of fashion, and with them those Hispanic faculty members who were appointed on non–tenure track slots (most Hispanas hired then were not on tenure track). Once the overt demand for trainers of bilingual teachers ebbed, there was no rush to capitalize on the newly acquired talent and no efforts for retention were mobilized. This was another instance where the skills that the Hispanas brought with them (i.e., the knowledge of another language and culture, and in many instances expertise in areas of research that had not been explored by mainstream researchers) were essentially devalued and virtually ignored by academics.

Affirmative Action Policies and Their Impact

Affirmative Action policies are the response of public and private industry to the demand for greater opportunity for all Americans to participate in the pursuit of happiness, regardless of gender and color of skin. For many, AAP/EEO, as they are usually referred to, represent an encroachment on their ability to discriminate against those they do not want to incorporate into their midst. For others, it has been an opportunity to learn more about the "Others" and an opportunity to enlarge their sphere of action and knowledge. Affirmative Action policies have highlighted the need for institutions of higher education to make their campuses more reflective of the population at large and, specifically, to provide role models for all students in attendance. They have also created resentment among members of groups that have traditionally reigned supreme as far as access to jobs and career advancement is concerned. Thus, we are treated to the absurd notion of reverse discrimination and to the actual devaluation of the Hispanas' achievement by invoking that their presence is solely due to Affirmative Action policies. Many nonminority students and faculty as well as administrators are under the false assumption that Affirmative Action is a code for "underprepared" in the case of students, "not equally talented" in the case of faculty, and "not experienced enough" in the case of administrators. Their suspicion is borne out by the lack of inclusion of minorities into the social fabric of academia. Perhaps when routine inclusion rather than exclusion becomes the norm, the message will be conveyed that although minority group members may have originally been sought to comply with the law, after twenty years of testing their presence in majority campuses there is no question that they have a relevant and rightful place in academia. This recognition will also stem the devaluation of the Hispanas' background and contribution that is so prevalent in most campuses. The following quotes attest to the present state of affairs regarding AAP/EEO: "We are rarely considered as viable candidates in majority institutions" (from a President of a community college); "My peers are sometimes condescending and expect me to know all about 'ethnic' issues. I was told that as a 'minority' I would not get tenure and must not feel confident being in this institution" (from an Assistant Professor in a large, private research institution); "In many ways I feel typecast into 'affirmative action' and 'helping roles' " (from an Associate Dean in a private institution). What these quotes also reflect, in many instances, is the inability of academia to translate the intent of Affirmative Action policies into the actual experiences of the few Hispanas engaged in academic positions today.

RECOMMENDATIONS

The recommendations that follow are offered with the expectation that for those institutions that feel so inclined, they will pave the way to take that extra step toward increased inclusion and recognition of this rapidly growing segment of the population.

It is fairly evident that the climate for Hispanas in academia is lukewarm at best. It is also evident that unless something is done to remedy the lack of representation of this particular group in the very near future, the impact of its absence will be felt in major ways throughout the economy and at all levels of the educational enterprise. There is nothing new about this clarion call—it has been sounded before. What is new now is the very short time left for any ameliorating action to take place before it is too late. The 1960s witnessed in the passing of the Civil Rights Act the culmination of one hundred years of struggle—a struggle that focused on the improvement of conditions under which the Black population had been existing in the United States. The 1990s will come to be known as the decade in which Hispanic Americans made their presence known and acted upon—and the answers that will ensue will come not from altruism but mostly as a response to economic imperatives.

Given that humans are always historically situated, our understanding is determined by the conditions we are familiar with. The better we understand these conditions, the better equipped we are to act on them. In order to best understand the contributions that Hispanas bring to academia we must also understand some of the assumptions they bring with them. I have not met any self-respecting Hispana, in academia or elsewhere, who wants to be considered as an imitation of an Anglo woman. What we would like to see, however, is an acceptance of our differences without considering them as flaws that will eventually be discarded. There are areas in which our cultural traditions differ considerably from the Anglo Americans. Hispanic women are closer to the European than to the North American sense of femininity. Like the French, Hispanic cultures celebrate sexual difference rather than similarity within a framework of male/female complementarity. As a result, instead of seeking unqualified admission to male-dominated society, Hispanas try to seek ways in which the totality of society and its institutions can be organized so that they can accommodate women. Thus, it is not considered necessary for Hispanas to relinquish femininity in order to succeed. Unfortunately, this perception is often very threatening to Anglo-Saxon men and women who believe that autonomy and femininity are antinomic concepts. As a result, Hispanas are viewed as flirty, not serious minded, and not autonomous enough to warrant inclusion into their midst. Within the academic arena, we find that Hispanas fail to see or receive credit for their accomplishments and that they tend to undervalue their own work and exaggerate the quality of work being done by men. They do so because they see their work as a contribution to shared understanding and not as individual achievement to be claimed and protected. This kind of thinking stems from being socialized in a society that does not emphasize or reward stark individualism. These are strong cultural values that prevail, and they are usually misinterpreted by unsuspecting Anglos. As for the tenuous presence of Hispanas in academia, it would be useful for institutions to think in terms of what conditions are keeping Hispanas in such low profile, rather than assuming that there are simply not enough of them out there.

The recommendations that follow reflect the confidence that the status of Hispanas in academia can be greatly improved and that the resulting payoff represents gains for all involved. To make them more manageable, I have grouped the recommendations by areas of intervention, namely, Faculty, Graduate and Undergraduate Students, and Administrative Personnel.

Faculty Positions

1. First and foremost, there is a need for institutions to do more research regarding their own standing as employers of Hispanas and to include disaggregated institutional data in their annual Affirmative Action reports. Such reports should be readily accessible to other constituents of academia, including Hispanas themselves.

2. In order to incorporate Hispanas into the fabric of the academic department or faculty where they are based, it is imperative that "buddy systems" be established to ease the newly employed into the grooves of academia. Through these people the Hispana will discover what avenues will best lead toward achieving her professional goals while maximizing her contribution to the institution. The buddy can be another faculty member who shares the same specialty field as the Hispana; it does not need to be another Hispanic person. In fact, it probably should not be, since most Hispanas in academic positions have not been there long enough to have already mastered "learning the ropes" themselves.

3. Recognize the varied nature of the Hispanic experience. Not all Hispanas look alike or speak with the same accent. Not all of them are called Maria. They have varied backgrounds and experience; do not try to pigeonhole them into the straightjacket of the all-encompassing "Hispana."

4. Recognize that the nature of research topics that interest some Hispanic faculty members may stem from their closer knowledge of a particular population. Thus, they may be more inclined to perceive issues and utilize paradigms that may not occur to Anglo professionals. To dismiss them as untested and unorthodox is to lose a tremendous source of innovative thinking and data interpretation.

5. Identify experts in different fields who are familiar with trends in other cultures and who can read research written in another language—in this case, Spanish—whether they are within the institution or outside. Far too often, work undertaken by the Hispana is devalued because there is no knowledge of the themes she is dealing with or of her body of underlying assumptions, if they happen to be rooted in the Hispanic culture.

6. In judging research proposed by Hispanas in areas related to the Hispanic experience, engage members of the community of scholars who know the assumptions from which the data are examined and who can make an informed judgment as to the validity of the premises.

7. Instill this same perception in people who handle grants money at the institutional level. There seem to be too many instances of failure to recognize the important nature of research topics brought forth by Hispanas, with the ensuing denial of funds for its undertaking.

8. Encourage faculty members in all fields to include Hispanic authors in their assigned readings. For those students who can read them in Spanish, it is a joy that boosts self-esteem; for those students who cannot, translations may be available that will allow them to read and understand, enriching their cultural understanding in the process.

9. Do not assume that because someone is Hispanic she is solely interested in Hispanic issues. In some instances, she may not be even slightly interested. Do not take her field of specialization for granted,

and resist the temptation of assigning her the role of Residing Campus Hispana.

10. If you are interested in the retention of Hispanas as faculty members, keep their advising loads at the same level as their peers even if their advice is being requested by the whole Hispanic student body. Avoid dropping all Hispanic students and their problems at their door.

11. Avoid falling into what a member of a research institution called "the policy of exclusion"—that is, looking at a resume and finding reasons to exclude the applicant rather than looking for reasons for inclusion—when Hispanas apply for faculty positions.

12. Do not expect to hire only Hispana superstars. There are many competent, hard-working Hispanas who shun the limelight and who are just as competent as most of the faculty that compose the backbone of most of our campuses. There is ample room for low key, consistent faculty members in any campus.

13. Be aware of the "glass ceiling" imposed on Hispanas once they are employed. Encourage and seriously consider their capabilities even when they steer themselves into career paths away from teaching, such as administration or research.

14. Insure that appointments of newly inducted Hispanas are routed through the tenure track. This will insure not only a firmer commitment from both the institution and the faculty member, but it will also relieve new faculty of the anxiety of reapplying for the position every Spring term, unable to tell whether she will be teaching next fall or not, unable to adequately plan her courses or research.

15. Do not devalue their personhood by continually mispronouncing and misspelling their names.

16. Beware of the token syndrome. No Hispana will ever be able to represent the totality of the Hispanic experience, nor should she be placed in a position where she is expected to. Hire more of them so that the diversity shines through.

17. Make a special effort to engage Hispanas in everyday, informal contacts. You will be surprised to find out how many things you have in common and how many things you can learn from each other.

Graduate and Undergraduate Students

1. Recognize that some of the overtly passive attitudes of the Hispanic female students may stem out of fear of being ridiculed because of accent or background assumptions.

2. Engage them in class discussions by calling on them often, asking questions, and responding to their comments. Concentrate on their contribution rather than on their linguistic delivery. If needed, offer them

individual assistance outside the classroom, if you do so for other students.

3. Allow room for humor in the conduct of discussions, since humor is used in Hispanic cultures as one of the avenues for dealing with confrontations—winning your case without crushing your opposition's ego. Thus, laughter on the part of Hispanas does not necessarily signal undervaluing of the theme or a lighthearted approach. A smile does not always represent acquiescence.

4. Provide enough role models for the Hispanic American students by employing and granting more visibility to Hispanas in faculty and administrative roles, not by overloading the lonely Hispana appointee.

5. Use the current crop of Hispanic students as a source for future faculty and administrative personnel.

6. Do not assume that all Hispanas bring into the classroom the same educational background, or that because they are Hispanas they must not have accomplished levels of attainment comparable to those of mainstream students.

7. Be aware that many Hispana students are struggling with economic and social barriers that detract from their ability to devote all their attention to their studies, and thus they may take longer than mainstream students to complete their degrees.

8. Make an effort to correctly identify Spanish names. It is very aggravating and oppressive to be dismissed as Maria when your name is Marta or Josefa. Ask the student for the correct pronunciation of her name and practice it until it is mastered. Require the same from fellow students and avoid the consistent misspelling of names. Recognize that Hispanas arrange their names differently and abide by it.

9. Be aware that some of the Hispanas in your classroom are facing personal conflicts stemming from the fact that they are becoming more educated than their spouses or significant others and that they may be unconsciously sabotaging their own progress.

10. Recognize that for Hispanas the ideology of feminism as espoused by Anglo women may not be the answer. That does not mean that we are not aware or that we do not understand levels of male oppression within our social milieu—we are just trying to deal with it within a framework that makes sense from our own set of cultural assumptions.

11. Help the students in their quest for a comfortable niche on campus by sharing with them perceptions and experiences that exemplify the essence of "Anglo college culture" and how can they best adapt it to their own styles.

12. Remember that cultural differences are reflected in body language. Learn to read the Hispanas' body language as accurately as you read Anglo body language.

13. Consider the establishment of a truly multicultural center wherein faculty and students can learn about other's cultures and dispel unfounded fears about each other.

14. Recognize and avoid veiled discrimination in action and in speech.

Administrative Positions

1. Encourage mainstream administrators to think of Hispanas when selecting individuals to be groomed for top administrative positions.

2. Train grants management personnel on multicultural approaches to research and the diversity of underlying cultural assumptions that are expected from a multicultural faculty, so that they do not automatically discount them when approached for funding.

3. Offer the opportunity for staff to attend seminars on cultural diversity and its impact on the quality of the campus climate for all.

4. Make allowances for and encourage Hispanic alumnae to visit the campus and address incoming students, to recruit other students, and to help with mentoring when appropriate. Not all the role models need to be academicians.

5. Allow funding for peer-mentoring systems to be established among Hispanas. That way the needy students can also engage in peer mentoring without impairing their ability to earn some very needed money.

6. Sponsor Hispana faculty members to offer institutionwide seminars on topics in their specialty, not just Hispanic issues.

7. Encourage department heads to revise their curricula and foster inclusion of works that incorporate the achievements of Hispanas in a variety of fields into the body of literature that all students are responsible for, not just those in Hispanic Studies Department.

8. Do not assume that Hispanics talking in Spanish among themselves are deliberately excluding you or talking about you. Most of the time they will be happy to translate and include you in the conversation. By the same token, remember to include them in your English conversations.

Conclusion

Perhaps by taking these and other steps we can find the initiative to reshape the world of academia and its politics in a manner that incorporates, rather than neglects, the sociopolitical dimensions of the Hispanas' presence and expertise on campuses around the country. This may require the reintegration of a male-oriented academic model into a more encompassing model—one that can accommodate a greater range of diversity—but it is by no means an insurmountable task.

8

Xenophobia or Xenophilia? Hispanic Women in Higher Education

Anita Leal and Cecilia Menjivar

INTRODUCTION

According to the Bureau of the Census, there were over 10 million Hispanic women, or 51.4 percent of a total of 20,076 million Hispanics, living in the United States in 1989. Hispanic women generally are lumped together under this generic label with virtually no attention to intragroup distinctions. The work done by H. Amaro, N. Russo, and J. Pares-Avila on Mexican, Puerto Rican, and Cuban women's mental health needs is an important exception (1987). The paucity of comparative intragroup studies of Hispanic women belies the diversity of their psychological and sociological reality (Amaro and Russo 1987).

This failure to consider intraethnic differences among Hispanic women is especially notable in institutions of higher learning. Even though federal law requires that universities and colleges engage in Affirmative Action programs, eligibility in university minority group programs for Hispanics often depends on Spanish surname as the primary qualifying attribute. Although statistics on specific racial/ethnic groups must be reported, legal requirements do not include information on racial/ethnic affiliation and self-identification, language preference, length of time in the United States, or other sociocultural factors.

The purpose of this chapter is to identify and discuss critical issues that emerged from an exploratory study of the perceptions of two subgroups of Hispanic women in higher education toward each other. Two subgroups of Hispanic women were identified for the study, results of which follow a review of literature. "Latina" refers to Hispanic women born and/or raised in the United States; "Latin American woman" refers to women born and raised in a Central or South American country. The focus of this chapter is on ethnic identity, networking, and mentorship of Hispanic women involved in higher education as graduate students and as faculty and their attitudes toward their educational experience and toward each other.

ETHNIC IDENTITY

The meaning of "ethnic identity" has undergone modification over time. However, the definition revolves to a greater or lesser degree around three dimensions: (1) endogenous aspect, or how individual members of the sociological group perceive themselves; (2) exogenous aspect, or how members of the group perceive themselves as distinguished from others; and (3) reality aspect, or objective aspects such as cultural history and cultural and language characteristics (Moore 1990).

S. Keefe and A. Padilla have defined ethnic identification as "self-identification among group members as well as their attitude towards affiliation with one ethnic group and culture as opposed to another group and culture" (1987, p. 8). There is virtually no research and literature on ethnic identity and group affiliation of subgroups of Hispanic women in higher education as a separate area of study.

Hispanic Heterogeneity

Although the term "Hispanic" is used in this chapter because of its general recognizability, it must be remembered that scientific and political limitations and controversy surround the use of this term (Hayes-Bautista 1980). This umbrella term and its parallel counterpart, "Latino," have been used to refer to Mexican Americans, Puerto Ricans, and Cuban Americans, collectively. The label is considered by many Latino scholars as euphemistic in intent and origin and as externally imposed rather than reflective of the identity of the collectivity (Padilla 1985).

In fact, Moore (1990) questions whether or not there actually is a collective Hispanic identity. She writes that " 'Hispanic' and 'Latino' have nothing to do with ethnic identity as it has been traditionally conceived, but they have a lot to do with the changing situation of Chicanos, Puerto Ricans, and other Hispanics locally, regionally, and especially nationally" (p. 44). She continues, "until recently Mexican Americans,

Puerto Ricans, and other Hispanics have had little similar experience either of urban mixing or of the need for coalition politics" (p. 45).

The largest segment of the Hispanic group, according to the Bureau of the Census, is people of Mexican origin (12.6 million), followed by Puerto Ricans (2.3 million), Cubans (1.1 million), Central and South Americans (2.5 million), and 1.6 million others, a growing residual category of people who identify generally as Hispanic, Spanish, Spanish American, and so forth.

Moore comments on the identity of Americans of Mexican origin, stating that "it is almost certain that Mexican Americans have the most complex history of all, and are the least likely to opt for a collective Hispanic identity" (1990, p. 35). As a result of the diversity of the Mexican American collectivity, Moore continues, "the Census had to include at least three self-identifiers for persons of Mexican origin—'Mexican American,' 'Chicano,' and 'Mexican' " (p. 35).

Use of Spanish Language

The relationship between language use and ethnic identity is important to understand. L. Estrada's study (1984) revealed that while 75 percent of the Hispanic population reported some degree of Spanish language usage, English dominant bilingualism was the most common type of language usage. Mexican Americans had the lowest rate of Spanish language usage.

O. Espin (1987) reported that the Spanish language may remain the language of emotions even if fluency in the Spanish language is lost. Furthermore, bilingual Spanish speakers who did not feel proficient in the Spanish language appeared withdrawn or reluctant to interact when faced with the expectation of communication in that language. Thus, there are both cognitive and affective implications of language dominance among Hispanic women. Clearly, as Espin points out, self-esteem can be inextricably connected to language, given that Spanish language use in the United States carries a shadow of stigma.

Migration

Related to issues of ethnic identification are effects of migration. H. Amaro and N. Russo (1987) explored the effect of migration on Latin American women who came to study or work in the United States. In their generative study, they found that "when a migrant comes from a country where she belongs to the racial majority, or where, as in Latin countries, racial mixtures are the norm, the experience of turning into a minority in the United States and encountering overt racial discrimination becomes a disorienting experience" (p. 493). Thus, we could expect that the alienation experience for Hispanic women would differ depending on their migration experience.

HISPANIC WOMEN IN HIGHER EDUCATION

The little information that exists about Hispanic women in higher education is very informative. Further, studies typically report female and male Hispanic faculty statistics as a combined figure with no subgroup distinctions. For example, T. Escobedo (1980) reported that 1.4 percent of available full-time faculty positions in universities and colleges were held by Hispanics, and of these, only 0.4 percent were held by Hispanic women. Furthermore, she reported that based on 1978 statistics, only 367 tenured and 486 nontenured professorship positions were held by female Hispanics.

F. Ortiz's (1988) study of Hispanic women in higher education focused on undergraduate and graduate students in four public institutions in California. She reported that the relatively few Hispanic women who were enrolled in graduate school majored in the humanities and liberal arts. This included education, social work, psychology, and foreign languages.

According to C. Johnson (1989), the number of Hispanic women receiving Ph.D. degrees increased from 20.1 percent in 1975 to 45.7 percent in 1986, for a total of 567 Hispanic women Ph.D.s in 1986. Furthermore, the graduate women in Ortiz's study found themselves without peer or faculty guidance. Overall, the women in Ortiz's study related feelings of isolation and alienation from faculty as well as feelings of lack of support. Many of them exercised the option to remain isolated and aloof in their professional contexts as a way of coping with their alienating situations.

NETWORKING IN HIGHER EDUCATION

M. Welch (1980) defined "networking" as a communication-linking structure that develops contacts for information, advice, and moral support toward career advancement. The importance of professional networking is acknowledged as an integral part of men's career trajectory. Academicians in general rely on professional networks for visibility as well as for information about current developments. Yet only recently has the importance of networking for women's professional enhancement received serious consideration. This is due mostly to the absence of networking among women and their exclusion from men's networks.

The exclusion of women from both formal and informal networks in higher education is clearly recognized as a structural barrier to their professional advancement. What develops instead are qualitatively different networking patterns among women in higher education. In her study of professional networks of forty-seven female and forty-three male junior faculty in psychology departments in sixty universities, S. Rose (1985) discovered that women had weaker collegial ties with their previous institutions than did men. Furthermore, "over 90% of the women had two or more same-sex associates, and close to two-thirds had a higher-status woman in their network" (p. 545).

Networking among Hispanic Women

No published literature was found comparing subgroups of Hispanic women in their networking patterns in education. A. Aguirre's (1987) investigation of Hispanic faculty involvement in academe led him to the following conclusion: "it is not so much that Chicano faculty are peripheral to the academic enterprise, as much as the nature of their institutional activity depicts them as peripheral participants in academe" (p. 73). K. Simoniella's pilot study (1981) of professional women of Mexican origin included women who were professors. She concluded that the informal network systems in higher education were inaccessible to Hispanic female faculty.

Networking among ethnic women has received limited attention. M. Wilkerson (1984) noted that women of color have a long tradition of activist networks that serve to affirm ethnic identity as well as enhance communication. Yet E. Almquist (1984) noted that the extent to which minority women develop significant ties with each other is largely uninvestigated.

MENTORSHIP

Closely related to networking is mentorship. M. Swoboda and S. Milar (1986) described mentoring as "an ever-changing series of dyadic contacts in which each person plays the role of mentor or mentee to differing degrees in each dyad" (p. 11). Women, in general, have found effective grooming-mentor relationships to be particularly important to their upward career mobility. However, ethnic women are easily overlooked in academe because mentors often choose mentees of the same class, ethnic background, and gender (Swoboda and Milar 1986).

Barriers to mentoring of Hispanic female graduate students was the subject of study for R. Quezada, K. Loheyde, and M. Kacmaczyk (1984). They found that little cross-sex and crosscultural mentoring was available for Hispanic graduate students. Furthermore, they pointed out that Hispanic women may not identify as "sisters in a common struggle" (p. 238). No intragroup distinctions were made in this study.

While no studies of Hispanic women's networking patterns were found, Ortiz (1983) investigated "Hispanic-American" women's adaptation to organizational conditions as faculty of California colleges. From a sample of thirty Hispanic women (eight professors and twenty-two staff), peripheral participation in the organization stood out. Hispanic women were allowed to participate without rigid bureaucratic obstacles yet missed out on the socialization inherent in bureaucratic networking.

EXPLORATORY STUDY

Because of the lack of information on Hispanic women's intragroup attitudes toward and interaction with each other in higher education, using a snowball sampling technique we identified ten Hispanic women to interview by phone or in person. As mentioned earlier, we distinguished between two subgroups of Hispanic women: (1) "Latina" referred to Hispanic women born and/or raised in the United States, and (2) "Latin American woman" referred to women born and raised in a Central or South American country. The following questions were central to our study: (1) How is the higher education experience similar or different for Latina women compared to Latin American women? (2) What are Latina and Latin American women's attitudes toward each other? (3) To what extent do these two subgroups of Hispanic women network?

The ten subjects were between the ages of twenty-seven and fifty-five. Six subjects were doctoral students in public universities. Three subjects were tenure track faculty members in public universities; five were from universities in the West; one was from a public university in the Southwest; and one from a private university in the East.

The promotional status of the tenure track faculty women was as follows: two assistant professors without tenure, one associate professor with tenure, and one full professor with tenure. Of the doctoral subjects, three were all-but-dissertation status, two were third-year students, and one was a second-year doctoral student. The subjects' areas of study included education, sociology, Chicano studies, foreign languages, counseling, psychology, anthropology, civil engineering, linguistics, and French literature.

Ethnic Identity

In general, ethnic identity as a concept was of more interest to Latinas than to Latin American women. The Latin American women questioned the appropriateness of the concept as it applied to them. These women found the analytical subgroup distinctions of Latin American versus Latinas as disagreeable and confusing. Four of the six doctoral subjects who were born in Latin America identified primarily as Caucasian and secondarily as Latin Americans. The Mexican-born doctoral student who identified as Mexicana, that is, Mexican, said that she felt split in her ethnic identity. She enjoyed Latin American art, culture, and theater as opposed to Chicano culture. Yet she stated, "I learned what being a Mexican was really about by networking with Chicanos here in the United States." She stated that in Mexico, the U.S. Hispanic minority group is "disdained, held in contempt and looked down upon because of class issues." She stated, "as I came to interact with Chicanos, I learned to appreciate the effects of their history of oppression and racism in this country. I now relate to both cultures." The other Latin American doctoral student born in Puerto Rico identified as a Puerto Rican. She explained, "on official forms I have been marking off Hispanic because someone in my university told me that is what I am."

Two of the four Hispanic faculty women were born in the United States and described their background as "working class." They identified strongly as Chicanas. The two remaining Hispanic faculty women identified equally strongly as Puerto Rican. One faculty woman who identified as Puerto Rican said she was of "mixed ancestry because only one of my parents is Puerto Rican." She described her family background as middle class with professional occupations and some college education. She said she faced discrimination in an interesting way because she did not look "Hispanic enough." She stated that although she is completely fluent in the Spanish language, when she was interviewed for faculty positions interviewers appeared disappointed in her appearance. She felt this was because she does not have what are frequently considered "Latina stereotypical physical features." She stated that she identifies strongly with the island of Puerto Rico as well as with its language and culture.

The other Puerto Rican professor stated:

I really see myself as a Puerto Rican and as a Latin American. I feel like I am a Puerto Rican immigrant even though I have lived in this country for over 30 years, since I was four years old. No soy gringa. I know I am a part of this body politic, pero soy gringa.

Overall, the ethnic identity of this sample of Hispanic women demonstrated a relationship between class and ethnic identification. Women born in Latin America who were of middle- and upper middle-class parents identified as Caucasian rather than with a specific ethnic group. On the other hand, the Chicana and Puerto Rican women in our sample clearly identified with their respective ethnic groups. Furthermore, in contrast to Latina women, Latin American women in our sample did not identify as "women of color" or as "minority group members," with the exception of the Mexican born doctoral student.

Networking

A significant finding in this exploratory study is related to the lack of networking between Latinas and Latin American women. The Chicana assistant professor said that her most important network "is Chicano." While she does network professionally with both male and females crossing racial and ethnic boundaries, she relied primarily on her Chicano network for professional and psychological support. She stated, "the failure of Latin Americans and Chicanos to interact is because of differences in class identity and class consciousness." The other Chicana professor stated, "I don't trust Latin American women. They are class-conscious conservatives. I also feel a barrier with white women . . . unless they are radical in some way." She networks at her university primarily with Chicanos. She said there were no Latin American faculty at her university. She said that she identifies with women of color because they have a "sense of equity, justice, and a palatable ideology."

The Puerto Rican assistant professor said that she had neither the time nor money to network within professional organizations in her area of study. Professionally, she interacts primarily with Puerto Ricans and "Anglos." Her strongest professional and supportive network consisted of Puerto Rican women in Puerto Rico. She stated, "Chicanos are indifferent to me, especially among faculty. . . . I feel like a pariah in my institution."

The Puerto Rican doctoral student felt that her primary network consisted of "Hispanic professionals of diverse background." She said that she helped form a multicultural professional organization in her community. She indicated that while she was in the Southwest she did not interact with Chicanos because "we were different." Now, however, she described her network as multicultural. She expressed a need to interact with Hispanic scholars and felt this was a void in her personal and academic life.

The Puerto Rican associate professor networked primarily with Latin Americans and Chicanas socially. Her strongest network was in graduate school. There, she interacted with and gained support primarily from white feminists. She stated that this was "the key in my networking and my strongest network." She said, however, that she felt that she must educate white feminists at times. She also shared an identity with Latino males "unless they espouse sexism. . . . I have to educate them too." She felt isolated from her professional networks. "I don't feel well connected. My perception is that others are better connected. Isn't this the paranoia of academe?" In her opinion, a common "ideology is the basis for networking, and my ideology, in part, is white feminism. I feel alone in my academic position except for one close female colleague who identifies as 'Latina.'"

The Latin American women born in South America all agreed that they did not network with Latinas, in particular Chicanas. They were in an academic setting in the West where the predominant Hispanic group is of Mexican origin or Chicano. Thus, it is to this group that they referred in their interviews.

One Latin American woman indicated that she "has never had a chance to meet or talk with a Latina." Her strongest network is with "Latin Americans and some Americans." She believed that one of the reasons for the lack of communication between Latin Americans and Chicanas was differences in language, culture, and ethnic identity. Another Latin American doctoral student said that she networked with other Latin Americans and some Americans. Part of her professional network included many male "international" students. While she did not network with Chicanos professionally, she had interacted with Chicano secretaries and gardeners at her institution. She found that language was the main obstacle in communicating with Chicanos. Her experience was that the Chicanos wanted to speak English and seemed embarrassed to speak Spanish. She felt that "Chicanos are prejudiced toward Latin Americans and exclude them socially."

Another Latin American doctoral student networked mostly with Latin Americans and Americans and did not network with Chicanos. She asserted that language was the foremost barrier to communication. "I choose not to socialize on the basis of language and culture, not nationality." She said it was easier for her to socialize with "an American who has lived in Latin America and speaks Spanish than with a Chicana who will not speak Spanish."

The Puerto Rican doctoral student also said that she did not want to network with Chicanas. She said she did not consider herself as "belonging to the same category as Chicanas." She felt she had more in common culturally with Cubans. Her professional network consisted of Americans and her social networks of Latin Americans. There were few opportunities for her to interact with Chicanos.

One notable exception to the lack of networking between Latina and Latin American women was the Mexican doctoral student. She felt that Chicanos reached out to her when she first came to the United States and helped her. There were so few Hispanics in the Midwest that she appreciated the friendship. Now all of her networks have merged into one, with her primary network being feminist women of color.

Mentoring

Because networking and mentoring are so closely tied, we asked our subjects about their mentoring experiences. While the doctoral Hispanic women reported they had mentors, the Hispanic faculty members reported this did not carry over from their graduate experience. As faculty, they felt isolated even if they had not felt so in graduate school.

The four Latin American doctoral students said that they had white male mentors. Furthermore, they reported a satisfactory experience with these mentors. The Puerto Rican doctoral student said that this topic was a very sensitive one for her. She had a white male mentor in graduate school to whom she had been assigned. She had difficulty relating to him because of his lack of interest and knowledge about her area of study. She felt she was a failure in the mentoring relationship. She felt that her doctoral studies had suffered and her dissertation had been delayed because of this unsatisfactory relationship.

The Mexican doctoral student also reported lack of mentoring experiences in graduate study. She voiced a lack of substantive and emotional support from her all-white male committee. They did not have an interest in her topic. As a result she was unable to complete her dissertation.

Among the faculty women, one Chicana professor said that she had had a white female mentor who "toughened up" her female doctoral students and had the reputation of taking only "strong women who were tigers" to work with her. She has had no mentors during her tenure as a professor. She said, "I have struggled every step of the way."

One Puerto Rican professor reported a similar experience. She had a strong white female mentor who was "very tough." The other Puerto Rican professor said she had had an "Anglo male mentor" who strongly identified with the Chicano culture. She felt, therefore, that he went out of his way to identify with her, making their relationship a very supportive one.

CONCLUSION

Based on both the literature and the results of our exploratory study, it is clear that there is reason to believe that Latina women and Latin American women in higher education do not spontaneously network or mentor each other. This situation exists for several reasons. It is not only because of class or ideological differences, but perhaps because of a lack of understanding of the other's experience. What emerges is a pattern of alienation of Hispanic women in higher education not only from the institution itself but from each other as well.

While it is true that there are variations in language preference, racial and ethnic identification, historical experience in the United States, as well as social class differences among Hispanic women, it is these factors precisely that can either positively or negatively affect communication between them. Hispanic women are not a monolithic or homogeneous group; they are as complex and diverse as the sociological group of Hispanics to which they belong.

Hispanic women may neither fear or be friendly with each other; instead, they merely may not understand the lens through which the other views their world. New awareness of intraethnic identity differences requires crossing boundaries. It is this sort of awareness that will insure the success of Hispanics in higher education.

Further study of networking patterns among Hispanic women in higher education will insure their retention and ultimate success. Institutions of higher learning should reexamine their Affirmative Action programs. They need to take into consideration the diversity of Hispanics as they seek to culturally diversify their institutions.

IV

International Perspectives on Minority Women and Higher Education

Part IV gives an international flavor to the issue of the roles of minority women in higher education. Because we have become a global interactive system with a global economic base, it is appropriate to take a world view as we try to understand the role of minority women in higher education. Dee Aker looks at the role women in higher education can take in supporting women throughout the world. She suggests that by bringing the ivory towers to the village streets, women in higher education can have a tremendous influence on the development of women as well as that of the country in which they work together.

Martha Tyler John emphasizes the need for women in higher education to become role models for women in developing nations. Recommendations are made by John regarding policies that would encourage the development of role models for young women in developing nations. Roberta Weil gives insight into the current role of Chinese women in higher education in China. She states that Chinese women believe that equal opportunity for higher education does not exist.

9

Academic Role Models Needed for Females in the Third World

Martha Tyler John

The world community must deal with a challenging, changing society, and the contributions of all people are needed if solutions are to be found to the complex issues surrounding us. Environmental deterioration and the problems of hunger and poverty are so severe that our best efforts will be needed to solve them. Indeed, the use of science and technology will be necessary if we meet and solve the ecological and human problems of the twenty-first century. It will require the creativity and commitment of 100% of the population; not just the 50% that are male. While crucial issues like those mentioned are present throughout society, they are especially pressing in less developed countries in the Third World. It is in these countries that the urgent need for improving human resources demands the most extensive use of talents and skills, and the use of the abilities of all their citizens.

One can use African Third World countries as representatives of the general condition in which less developed countries find themselves. In different parts of Africa there have been real difficulties involving food production and distribution during recent years. Several times during the last ten years, major famines have devastated whole groups of people. Problems of infrastructure and transportation shortfall have made it almost impossible for other nations to provide relief for the stricken areas. Predictions indicate that such problems are not over but may, in fact, become even worse in the future. One of the conditions the predictors consider is population growth.

The population in Third World Africa is growing rapidly. Nigeria and Kenya, for example, have two of the highest birth rates in the world. The difficulties that will be encountered with the population predicted for the year 2000 can only be imagined with dread, especially when one considers the age level of the population. The continent of Africa currently has the youngest population on earth, and the young people in any country are those that are capable of producing more children.

As the population increases, the need for food, an efficient work force, and effective technology to solve the problems of food production and distribution become even more pressing. In reality the 45% of the population that are young people will all be needed as competent workers if any quality of life is to be enjoyed in Third World countries. It will be disastrous if half this group, the female half, does not acquire skills to assist in developing the country's resources to meet the challenge of the twenty-first century.

It is the population now growing up, this zero–fourteen year-old group, that must be convinced to develop specific skills; and it is the young women of the group who are most in need of special encouragement. A redefinition of roles and the use of new skills will be needed. J. Kagan (1987, p. 53) says, "When the time comes to list the momentous changes of the twentieth century, high on the list will be the massive redefinition of the role of women." While he is probably referring to Euro-Western cultures primarily, the roles of women are being redefined in the Third World also. Even so, the female scholars who can serve as role models for promoting and encouraging change in the Third World are few. What is needed are female role models who can be seen to be truly scholarly and fully women at one and the same time. Some do exist and these few can serve as examples, but more are needed if little girls growing up in Africa see areas like computer science, chemistry, or banking as having possible career potential for them.

SOCIAL LEARNING AND MODELING

Much of what a child or young person learns is learned in a social context. The child observes behavior, often identifies with an adult who serves as a model for the behavior, and then imitates the behavior him/herself. "Both imitation and identification refer to the tendency for a person to reproduce the actions, attitudes, or emotional responses exhibited by real-life or symbolic models" (Mischel 1970, p. 28). "In human societies, the provision of models not only serves to accelerate the learning process but also, in cases where errors are dangerous or costly, becomes an essential means of transmitting behavior patterns" (Bandura and Walters 1963, p. 52). We learn vicariously; that is, we observe another person in a situation similar to our own and from it determine the reward system associated with the situation or the individual's behavior in the circumstance. We then decide upon our own course of action, having learned from another person's experiences. If a society wishes females to behave in a specified way, then providing models, that is, females who already behave in this manner and who are rewarded by society for the behavior, is an efficient way to obtain the desired behavior.

There is more to developing positive behavior than simply providing a person who can serve as a model, however. Incentives for preferred behavior must be designed, also. In most societies there are systems for rewards already established and these would need to be taken into account if one were to devise an effective modeling situation. Furthermore, the type of person that could serve as a model, one whom young girls would wish to imitate, would also need to be explored. What do we look for in a person that might be described as a model? There are several qualities to look for in the model, and different types of models that may be more or less effective in varying situations. Certain characteristics seem to be sought generally such as high status, nurturance, and future control. Status may not be the same for all individuals. For example, a scholar might see a professor or teacher as a status figure, while an athlete might see an Olympic medalist or a Hall of Fame person as having more status for them. Nurturance is often thought of in mother/child relationships, but a more generic definition could apply to providing sustenance or warmth or support when it is needed. Probably for most adults this broader definition is more useful. Future control can be seen as the ability of the model to provide positive reinforcement or to withdraw reinforcement. Reinforcement can take on many different forms. For example, the ability of the person to write a positive, influential recommendation for a desired position, to make proper introductions, or to obtain access to the training that the individual needs are all types of future control that will in some direct way affect his/her life.

If females are to participate fully in the development of their countries, they will need to become skilled in the sciences and in areas that have previously been male dominated. Even in so-called developed countries this is difficult, however. Warren Bennis and Burt Nanus (1985) interviewed 100 people in the United States including governors, senators, labor leaders, and executives of large companies. They looked for patterns that would explain the success of this group. "They were right-brained and left-brained, tall and short, fat and thin, articulate and inarticulate, assertive and retiring, dressed for success and dressed for failure, participative and autocratic" (p. 23). Eighty-eight of these leaders were white males, six were women, and six were black men, "reflecting the legacy of sexism and racism in the corporate world" (p. 25). "In 1986, 698,600 women scientists and engineers were employed in the United States. This represents 15 percent of all scientists and engineers, up from 9 percent in 1976" (Malizio 1988, p. 3). Hiring females increased 6% in ten years. While this shows a trend in the right direction, it also indicates a need for programs in the United States to step up their efforts in the scientific and technological training of women. If this is true in a highly technological society, then the situation in Third World countries is undoubtedly at least as critical.

It would seem that one way to help women develop skills would be to provide models who have great skill in technological areas. For the girl child, the model would probably be more effective if the child could see a person who had many of the societally approved female characteristics, as well as the skill the growing child sought. "It is difficult to ignore the messages of your society—especially for young women, who are not usually the most confident of people, and for whom (unlike young men) being independent and arrogant is not held up as desirable" (Kagan 1987, p. 54). The messages of society are essential to the enculturation of the growing child, and if she/he is to become an acceptable member of the society, the clues must be interpreted carefully. The comparison between males and females can be seen clearly in the preceding statement. Young men are taught to be independent; young women are not. Are there other differences that might significantly affect the female's ability to participate in the advancement so much needed in Third World countries? How far-reaching are the differences in skills acquisition?

It would be useful to learn about the level of skills in Third World African countries for both males and females, especially those that are reflected in the younger population. In examining the level of skills that primary school children possess, one can extrapolate to the situation that might prevail in the future. Several studies have been done that have explored this variable, especially in the area of logical thinking. A summary of the results of these research efforts provides thought-provoking data.

RESEARCH PROVIDES INFORMATION

Jean Piaget, a Swiss psychologist, developed a number of logical thinking tasks and these have been explored with several populations of African children, as well as children in other countries around the world.

Piaget explored children's ability to classify objects and to determine superordinate and subordinate categories. He also examined the concept of conservation, which he defined as the ability to recognize the properties of a substance and not be fooled by a slight change in the appearance of the substance. For example, the child who conserves number recognizes that eight sweets in a group are the same as eight sweets in a long row. The child is said to conserve weight, for instance, if she/he recognizes that two balls of clay are the same weight when one is rolled into a sausage and when both balls of clay are the same round shape. The skill to carry out this type of mental operation is much needed in scientific fields and in working with changing technological systems. Sex differences in crosscultural studies in performance on Piagetian tasks similar to those described have been investigated by several researchers in Africa. A. Heron and M. Simonsson (1969) conducted logical thinking tasks with Zambian children. B. Bliss and E. Docherty (1979) explored conservation tasks with Yoruba children, and neither team of researchers found any significant differences between boys and girls in their ability to logically complete the tasks. However, in studying Ugandan children, B. Otaala (1973) stated that among his subjects the boys did "decidedly better than girls" (p. 71). He attributed this superiority to differences in upbringing, particularly the expected degree of compliance—the idea being that females apply strong compliance codes whereas males are expected to demonstrate more independence, up to a point. E. Bam (1982) found in research on Basotho children that there are "differences between the performance of the male and female subjects in the mass, weight, liquid and number experiments." No research data tell why this is so, but "it is common for boys to have greater freedom to play and explore away from the home than girls do and this practice may influence their responses in the conservation experiments" (pp. 90, 91).

In E. Fahrmeier's (1978) study of Hausa children in Nigeria, sex differences were compounded by age factors: Older boys tended to conserve more than older girls, but the younger boys were not superior to the younger girls. M. John, M. Dambe, S. Polhemus, and F. John (1983) in research in Botswana found that "males performed significantly better than females (at the .05 level). In classification the difference was not significant, but the percentage of females successfully completing the tasks was slightly higher than the percentage of males" (p. 234). In a study conducted in Swaziland by E. Nsibandze and M. John (1985) the male/female variable was again examined with young children. "A comparison was made between male and female pupils for the six tasks. The analysis indicated the differences between sexes were not statistically significant; however, the percentage of successful females was always less than the percentage of successful males" (p. 36).

In the studies cited here there is some conflicting evidence. However, where the researchers do find differences, they are in areas of interest to the scientific community. For example, in the research in Botswana the males outperformed the females on tasks like seriation and conservation of length, mass, and weight. Females outperformed males in conservation of number and did slightly better on classification tasks but not at a level of significance. These tasks were completed with 554 pupils between first and seventh standard (grade). The number of males and females in various age groups differed, so Cochran's Y was used to adjust for these differences and to compare proportions of males and females who successfully completed tasks.

It has been acknowledged that there is some conflicting evidence in the studies cited and that the level of differences obtained did not always reach a level of significance. Clearly, additional research is needed to provide a more definitive analysis of societal influence and a better basis on which to plan strategies for intervention. Given the information at hand, however, there is considerable evidence that at these young age levels male/female differences in ability are emerging. If this is indeed the case and if this logical operational difference continues, then the potential for equivalent productivity in the scientific world would seem open to question, at best. Early intervention and special efforts for providing females with the skills needed seem essential. Providing models who can demonstrate these skills and have prestige and future control potential seems equally essential.

POLICY IMPLICATIONS

Governments in the Third World recognize the importance of the participation of all citizens in the development of the countries. If a country values the involvement of women in the more technological areas of development, then policies will have to be developed that more directly indicate the female population in these areas. The special needs and responsibilities of the woman in the workplace will need to be addressed. For any real contributions to come from the female sector, there will have to be reward systems that allow for women to promote to higher-level jobs. P. Udokang (1985, p. 20) tells us that "the vast majority (75 to 90 percent) of assembly workers in the electronics industry around the world are women. Most of them are new entrants to the labor force, usually with some high school education." These are young women and the author tells us that by the time they are thirty they are no longer in the labor force. Low level jobs do not provide motivation for remaining on the job. A different set of rewards must be provided if any significant number of women are going to remain in school and eventually join the productive, working community.

If we are to produce scholarly models for the young female, some basic interventions are needed. Governments should develop policies that:

1. provide educational opportunities that are based on skills development for both males and females.
2. provide additional instruction for females in the math and science areas in primary grades (early intervention).
3. develop apprentice or internship programs for female students who show interest or aptitude in technology (use of nurturance).
4. allow leaves (once the female joins the work force) for pregnancies and birthing children without penalty or demotion.
5. provide a wage that is adequate to enable the mother to obtain child care services or provide day care centers that are expense free.
6. develop special skills renewal educational programs for females returning to the work force.
7. provide a truly equal opportunity for the female to advance in management (status, future control).

These general policy recommendations apply to any country in which there is need for a more effective work force.

In the Third World, the greatest hope lies in education, the best chance to improve the lot of rural (or urban) women. Curriculum developers working on new projects must now begin to design new approaches, departing from the traditional home economics and nutrition programs in favor of training women to become cash earners, business handlers, nutrition planners and farm and irrigation managers. (Chu 1985, p. 22)

They must take a new role in their societies and function as an efficient, knowledgeable part of the creative changes taking place around the world. Help from government and from those in the private sector who influence policy is needed if today's neophyte female scholars are to develop their potential fully. Once models can be readily identified by young women, the ongoing process of developing experts for Third World countries will become self-perpetuating. This would be highly desirable—a beginning solution to severe global problems.

10

Ivory Towers and Village Streets: An Essential Role for Women in Higher Education in Global Survival Issues

Dee Aker

INTRODUCTION

Women for thousands of years have been the repositories of survival knowledge and technology that acknowledge our interdependence on (and with) this planet. Women must now take care to see that this wisdom is incorporated in the teachings and in the functioning of institutions assigned to shepherd our conscious development, institutions that should be addressing our planetary survival.

In great measure the industrialized world, locked into patriarchal educational frames of reference, demands that we ignore natural relationships and place frenzied consumerism and competition over compassion and cooperation in our search for understanding. Simultaneously, many are attempting to steer the developing world down similarly unenlightened paths. They hold subjugation of others (defined so by ethnicity, gender, religion, or socioeconomic standing) or exploitation of things (i.e., animals or environments) as appropriate pursuits.

The cost of expending so much of our intellectual prowess on limited, self-serving ventures has left humankind at a critical juncture. Our central human challenge now is to revive a balanced, evolutionary search for empowering wisdom. This search could be aided by educational goals that are liberating, life enhancing, and gender inclusive.

Such goals imply reorienting ourselves and sculpting a different design for our educational institutions. They demand that we find a model or create a prototype that is free of the prevailing views in traditional academic circles, the ones equating difference with inferiority or superiority. Those views are most visibly reflected in the violent and selfish aspects of cultures everywhere, both in and out of ivory towers. This is the perspective of the system identified as the white male society (Schaef 1985).

Cultural transformation theory (Eisler 1988) holds that this is only one of two basic cultural or societal models that have been fundamental to humankind's development so far. The prevailing condition of ranking one-half of humanity over the other (and variations on that racist, sexist theme) is the dominator model. The other, the partnership model, is based on linking rather than ranking members of society.

The objective must be to loosen the grip of the predominate norm or paradigm. It has encouraged the technologies designed to destroy and dominate. Because women have more often nourished the seeds of the partnership model, women must try to create the critical mass needed to actualize a new paradigm, one that sustains and enhances life in its ecological, social, and spiritual evolution. Indications from history, current crossdisciplinary activities, and newly audible voices suggest that the recovery of an inspired educational vision will lead women and men to discover their immense power in sensitivity to the integral order of life in the universe.

There is a vital link between two human survival factors intrinsic to the historic role of women and the profound new role that women in higher education can play in the search for wisdom that leads to essential understanding and to global survival. That link has been made visible in the growing academic testimony coming from distinct fields of study.

Anthropological and archaeological evidence now confirms that it is humankind's ability to cooperate with one another, not dominate one another, that led to civilization. What allowed societies to advance and enabled a sense of community and self did not spring from nasty, brutish, argumentative displays of male bravado. It blossomed from cooperation, communication, and the ritual celebrations of life (Leakey and Lewin 1978).

Likewise, the growing evidence of a distinct, definable feminine moral development pattern identified through psychological and sociological research from Miller J. (1976) to C. Gilligan and J. Attanucci (1988) attests to a primary relationship, or way of interacting, with the world that has come to be uniquely associated with feminine gender.

While nurturance and cooperation, manifestations of this moral development pattern, are more aptly described as human traits (Morrow 1990), they have crossculturally been embodied and associated with the female gender for a long time. Because of this they have been discounted in most of recorded history by the reigning patriarchal systems, with the exceptions of aberrations and nonconformists such as saints and idealists.

The current endeavors to demarginalize women and the concerns of women through interactive women's studies, women in development projects, and crosscultural journalism have provided practical knowledge and unprecedented access to the previously "invisible and inaudible" women of the world. Arbitrary barriers have been crossed by women in and out of academia. These women have become involved in the economic, political, and family priorities of their sisters who are displaced or victimized. Neither group is as mute as before (Huston 1979; Overholt, C., Anderson, M., Cloud, K. and Austin, J. 1985; Carter 1989; and Hayslip, L. 1990). For increasing numbers of women, profound experiences of feminine strength, resilience, dignity, cooperation, and intimate knowledge of life's essentials have become as visceral as they have been cerebral in the past.

The historic human survival factors intrinsic to women concern their pivotal role in food production and in social reconstruction after political and/or cultural devastation. In spite of women's exclusion from official technical training or political power, women's ways often provide needed sustenance and clear a path for human recovery. The nearly universal relegation of women in recorded history to places where they are institutionally oppressed, educationally deprived, and legally abused has not stopped them from playing vital roles in community survival. At the core of their ability to achieve reconciliation are the seeds of the life-sustaining values that can revitalize education and its mission.

Before we clarify the specific values needed to create attentive and responsible institutions of higher education, it is appropriate to consider where higher education's priorities have taken it. The Western patriarchal educational focus on pragmatic, rational domination has not led to well-adjusted individuals or a healthy home planet. It has not prepared societies for dealing with current developments and opportunities. It does not appear that advanced centers of study have been nourishing or leading on a global scale or an individual one.

Educators and policymakers educated in the traditional patriarchal schools of thought have focused on systems that could manipulate the human element. They do not begin with a focus on human beings as a means of discovering the natural systems in operation. The traditional intellectual enterprise of differentiation cum fragmentation stunts all of us in our understanding of the larger spheres of influence and responsibility in which we are integral. Both genders have world views colored by the predominate values in their educational experience. It is important to examine our values, methods, and goals in education.

Narrowed interests for many in scholarly pursuits have boarded up the windows as well as locked the doors of their ivory towers. They no longer feel the winds of impact and chaos, even though these winds swirled out of their previous successes or excesses. These very winds could ultimately shake the towers to their foundations. Exclusion of part or all of any university community from the larger society, whether by self-limiting specialization or social custom or political act, has been extremely costly on a number of occasions.

The history of women and the history of the world demonstrate the absence of women in the decision-making processes that have created our present global crises, ecologically and socially. But women can no longer claim by virtue of their previous exclusion that they are not responsible for an alternative future. The alternatives are visible. They are particularly visible to women given the opportunity to study human evolution and consciousness.

The orientation to problem solving identified as feminine is not gender specific, nor is it always apparent in the lives of and research on women. It is, however, commonly observed in the manner in which women who have not been molded by a Western patriarchal form of education address problems of great, life-threatening magnitude. The voices and choices of women around the world are a major resource suggesting a transformational reconciliation with both the planet and its "other" inhabitants. Women in higher education inspired by some other, living on a distant village street, may be able to gain the strength and stamina needed to open the window and unlock the doors of higher education. We begin by looking back in time and across the world in this time to find our teachers. We listen to their individual stories as well as the statistics and reports about their worlds.

HISTORICAL PERSPECTIVES: WOMEN, FOOD PRODUCTION, SOCIAL RECONSTRUCTION, AND SURVIVAL

United Nations statistics indicate that women constitute one-half of the world's population, produce 70 percent of the world's labor, earn one-tenth of the world's income, and own less than one-hundredth of the world's property. Women comprise two-thirds of all illiterate people, and between one-third and one-half of all households are headed by women (The World's Women, 1991).

Women grow over half of the food worldwide. This is done with little technical advice (Tinker 1988), as men constitute the vast majority of technical advisors for food production and they do not communicate with women producers in most societies (Overholt, C., Anderson, M.,

Cloud, K., and Austin, J. 1985). In Africa, women produce 80 percent of the food but are not included in the economic planning, nor do they have input into developmental choices through legislative offices (with the outstanding exception of the new government of Yoweri Museveni of Uganda). The result has been tragic.

Without the input of the majority of producers, two major trends in agriculture continue to be assumed globally valid. They are large-scale commercialization and the growth of cash crops for export. Two of the most devastating policies endorsed by Third World governments are exactly these. (If we add militarism, tribalism, or nationalism and sexism as they are practiced on the global scale, not only do we have problems with starvation but our entire planet is in danger of annihilation). Food production policies that do not incorporate women's experience have encouraged the large-scale commercial endeavors for export crops that have taken away land historically used for food self-sufficiency in developing countries.

As the men owners of the land have received development funds and outsider technical advice, they have generally chosen to cultivate cash crops almost exclusively. The voice of the subsistence farmers, the women concerned with feeding their families, is not acknowledged. A film produced by OEF, Inc., called *Seeds of Promise* (1988), vividly illustrates this complication. John Bodley (1982) vividly illustrates the rampant, victimizing, short-sighted development policies in *Victims of Progress*.

Even in most societies where the role of female farmers is thought to be recognized, no real voice has been given to their concerns. For example, against the backdrop of land expropriation that was part of the upheaval in dictator Somoza's overthrow and the building of a new country, land reform practices have brought a double shift and a more demanding life to women in Nicaragua (Snapp 1988).

It is now estimated that about one-half of all households on this earth are headed by women without partners available to support them. This represents a common social responsibility for about a billion women, women who on the surface do not seem to have a lot else in common. They speak about 3,000 different languages and definitely do not represent a homogeneous cultural history, nor do they share a similar physical environment. The vast majority do have more in common, however. They suffer from some form of structural violence, violence resulting from the unequal power they have available to address their needs within their cultures (Hamilton 1987). They also choose to survive. We should not be dismayed that women have remained the true, sensitive agriculturalists and food producers in so many lands. We need only take responsibility to see that women's wisdom is no longer discounted and that conditions imposed by structural violence inherent in the dominator model cease. The poorest and least powerful of the world's people can teach transformational leaders about priorities.

ORGANIC PARTNERSHIP

The dualism currently perceived and encouraged especially in Western traditions between humanity and nature is not the historical reality of women. Our ancestors seemed to perceive humans to be an intrinsic part of nature and not, therefore, in ultimate control. Their ecological consciousness was participatory. This feminine relationship with nature was more of a partnership.

Marti Kheel (1988, p. 84) reminds us that for most of human history, lay women healers saw nature as their ally. With a holistic perspective that trusted nature, they employed many dimensions of their experience to help with healing. My own experience in working with the psychological issues of physically ill individuals in the 1970s gave me a transformational glimpse of what such holistic consciousness would mean to our well-being, physically, emotionally, and socially (Mundschenk 1977).

Perhaps women's participatory view of nature is most apparent in the context of the intertwined realities of production and reproduction. Maria Mies (1986, p. 16) calls production of sustenance "the production of life" and says that this organic partnership with nature lets women perceive the environment just as they conceive of their own bodies, as places in which life is "allowed" to grow.

This knowledge is not universally perceived any longer, however. Such a principle of creating and conceiving life is lost to the ecologically alienated, consumerist women of the world (Shina 1988, pp. 19–21). It therefore becomes essential that we in education learn from and then try to illuminate the wisdom of those not caught in the dichotomies, the reductionism, and fragmentation of nature. A prehistory, feminine, earth goddess empathy and the continuing relationship of many women in the Third World to food production remain part of the essential world knowledge to be tapped for a truly functional world view.

At the same time, it is important to question attitudes that disregard relationships with the land as well as other peoples who share this planet. There is increasing awareness that policies and tools not appropriate for women are just not appropriate policies (Maduro 1988, pp. 53–54). Our reaction time to this growing consciousness may be too slow without a concerted effort by those in education to disseminate the information more rapidly.

The violation of nature is closely linked to the marginalization of women. An increased respect for the "feminine" dimension of human experience may bring about an increased respect for nature, or vice versa. Women still intimate with nature act as intellectual repositories for a holistic ecological precondition that appears to be necessary for recovery and survival of nature. They are embodiments of the missing dimension in many attempts to solve societal and relational problems or to secure a viable global future. So many of our macroproblems have been created by the microsolutions, such as the environmental impact of everything from DDT to disposable baby diapers. This is the result of our fragmented approach to problem solving, one inherent in an isolated discipline approach to solutions.

BREAKING CHAINS WILL NOT BE EASY

Even a brief reflection on the cost of excluding women from participating, whether in governance of their plot of land or in their societies, suggests that it is time for a champion to appear and open the way for their inclusion. That champion should be institutions of higher education. Within those institutions, that leadership will come from those, regardless of gender, who see what the cost has been for ignoring or denying a valid aspect of human wisdom. However, it will not be an easy task for individuals or institutions; oppressive habits are quite entrenched.

Custom continues to dictate even after new research is available and laws have changed. Two relationships between women and the law reflect this. First, in many societies with laws prohibiting the oppression of women, these laws are just not upheld. Historic and current suppression and oppression of women are rooted in the patriarchal priorities of tribes, city-states, kingdoms, and nations that seek power over others. Given that limited self-interest, a second consequential factor is that the inclusion of women under law does not automatically mean the inclusion of "the feminine" in ways of relating to the world.

Recognition of woman's position, legally and legislatively, does not mean the rise of compassion, nurturing, or visions of unity. Even the "macho" paradigm can include women if only they follow the nationalistic, tribalistic, exclusive, adversarial customs and rules. Elizabeth and Victoria of England, Catherine of Russia, Golda Meir of Israel, Indira Gandhi of India, and the Iron Maiden Margaret Thatcher, all were locked into structural straightjackets of national security and identity when they chose their roles (Miche 1986).

The difficulties in spreading this basic orientation of recognition of women to others who are change agents is complicated by the lack of support or limited interests of institutions that should be supportive, such as religious or educational ones. Churches and religious institutions do not often model recognition of women as equally valued partners on

122 Perspectives on Minority Women in Higher Education

earth or in their paradises, either. Often we find great gaps between official policy and common practice in women's rights by religious establishments. In fact, women upholding their faith and choosing to work earnestly for abolition of slavery in the 1830s in the United States were, other than Quakers, the same ones not given equal rights of participation in their churches.

Women have continued to model the values espoused by their religious organizations. More specifically, the religious organizations have continued to espouse the values women often live by even if these institutions do not seem to embody them at times. In an interview with Sister Mary Hartman, who protested weekly in front of the American Embassy in Nicaragua over a number of years, it was clear that her convictions about the rights of freedom from harassment were for both the men and women of Nicaragua ("Women," Show 133, 1988). But Sister Mary Theresa Kane's plea in the same decade to Pope John Paul II that women of the Roman Catholic church be allowed to join the clergy did not suggest that tradition sees women as equally spiritual, wise, or free (*Women's Realities, Women's Choices* 1983, p. 356).

Women do not seem to be in line for equal participation and acceptance in their various roles and homes on this planet without a concerted effort to create a holistic community. The institutions of higher education can help change this. While women's studies have helped focus on women's realities and have led to reexamination of larger issues in our academic and social communities, there has not been a restructuring of knowledge to make it resonate with what have been identified as feminine perceptions of the world and partnership consciousness.

That awaits more than a discipline such as women's studies or programs for women in development. It is dependent upon an intellectual revolution that at its core is a new process, not a new field of endeavor.

NEW PATHS FOR HIGHER EDUCATION AND WOMEN IN HIGHER EDUCATION

Two issues are important in women's relationship with higher education. They will determine our commitment to it. The first concerns whether education can take a primary role in creating a viable global future. Without a transformation, it seems, education is destined to be a slave to the world it helped create, rather than a visionary leader. The second issue is women's involvement in the hallowed halls. Again, there are critical factors of empowerment and relevancy.

It will take a strong commitment and some real risk taking for educational institutions to do what governments and nations often find threatening: change, proactively and graciously and wisely! Widespread poverty and hunger, environmental and human degradation, the "successes" of industrialization that are so costly to life on earth, all are components of a macroproblem in which education has played, at best, a dubious role in recent history. Much of the education sought in institutions of higher learning prizes a compartmentalized knowledge based on reductionism and sustains obsessive consumerism while discounting altruism. That is not destined to lead us to survival.

The consequences of an education system that teaches that our human priorities are best met in high gross national production figures and not in relation to future generations' options for a healthy home on earth are already closing in on us. This early patriarchal foundation clearly spelled out a priority that distanced it from village streets. The good was to obtain power in little spheres of influence without regard for others; in fact, it was best to distance those obtaining higher education from those of lower education. It did not suggest there was responsibility for long-term or faraway consequences. Long term and far away have become immediate and close, however; it is necessary to reconsider our selective, self-centered educational priorities or, at the very least, see if they can be more inclusive.

Finding viable global solutions to the macroproblems created by this dominator model necessitates bringing together what have been long treated as two separate streams of scholarship and world views, both feminine and masculine ways of understanding and being. The futurist Hazel Henderson believes that the wisdom of an "ecologically-aware, androgynized planetary culture" (1988, p. 16) is already taking shape. While she believes that the "patriarchs . . . want to continue dominating the Earth, exploiting its forests, minerals and lands . . . (and) to put women back in the kitchen, the gay people back in the closet and the Blacks and Hispanics back at the end of the line," her "principle of interconnectedness" has the potential to "breakthrough" because we are aware that social orders that worked for only some people and at the expense of others have all failed (p. 17).

The elitist social order priorities of higher educational institutions have failed the larger society even when these institutions have been acutely aware of a crisis. This usually happens when a university chooses to teach from the accumulation of human thought without suggesting the responsibility that falls to the educated.

Too much of the pomp and circumstance in education is form without essence. Form without essence is one of the key issues for women involved with learning institutions. In order to participate at all, essential wisdom may be discounted or ignored so that an acceptable form or format is maintained by women in the system.

Although women had been more literate in secular society than men during the Middle Ages and to some extent cultivated women had been more valued during the Renaissance, by the 1700s the proper education for women was "one that would train women to obey and please our future husbands" (*Women's Realities, Women's Choices* 1983). When doors reopened to women a little in the 1800s, it was with restrictions. Colleges for women and women's admittance to previously all-male universities demanded that the male-defined curriculum be upheld. Certainly there was no recognition that women might bring something of value. Oberlin, one of the first colleges to accept women and the only one to accept Black women, stated the prevailing attitude with its announced purpose of "the elevating of the female character, bringing within the reach of the misjudged and neglected sex, all the instructive privileges which hither to have reasonably distinguished the leading sex from theirs" (Hogeland 1972).

Some educated women demonstrated a commitment to their own priorities and to their essential purpose for getting an education, regardless of the prescribed limits of higher education and the society. Half of the teachers who volunteered to teach freed children after the Civil War were women, both Black and White. These women were intimidated, whipped, raped, and killed, but they persisted (Lerner 1977). One freed and educated girl who would later speak of the potential for inclusive education was Anna Julius Cooper:

Now I claim that it is the prevalence of Higher Education among women, the making it a common everyday affair for women to reason and think and express their thought, the training and stimulus which enable and encourage women to administer to the world the bread it needs as well as the sugar it cries for. (Quoted in Loewenberg and Bogin 1976, p. 321)

For the most part, when women began moving into higher education in the 1800s it was not as a result of organized feminist or feminine appeals to the men running the institutions. Most were concerned with keeping their families functioning in a society beset with growing problems. They were accustomed to maintaining their "woman's place." But social conditions were such by the time of the Civil War that necessity led to some women joining the ranks of the physicians and the clergy. Even these women did not seek self-aggrandizement (Westervelt 1974, p. 30) or roles that could impact the institutions themselves. Certainly, no one remembered that women had been important in the faculties of medieval universities and convents in Europe or believed that they could ever stage a comeback in such roles.

In the 1940s a few voices in the educational wilderness questioned the assumption popular in most institutions of higher learning that women had little to offer "man-made civilization" (Ulrich 1941). Plato's inclusion of females as capable and just rulers because they, too, could understand the underlying harmony of the universe had been forgotten along the way in discussions of the classics (Martin 1982, p. 138).

This was one of those times when the purpose of education was again coming into question. It made the consideration of the relation of women to education all the more interesting. The discussion was over whether education was to doggedly emphasize information and "job preparation" or was to have a "human aim" and be a good preparation for individuals to participate fully in their own development and the affairs of the community and the nation.

Nearly fifty years later the question about the purpose and direction of education is still with us. So, too, is some doubt about women's relevancy in it. According to Elizabeth Janeway, author of *Powers of the Weak*, women's "lives are still regarded as irrelevant." (Janeway 1986). Statistics indicate that women are not making great inroads. Administrators involved in the University of California and University of Virginia studies of what needs to be done to diversify and enrich faculties said that "colleagues are satisfied with slow progress as long as they are not seen lagging behind other institutions" (McMillen 1987).

All of this reflects a sad role for an institution that should and could be visionary. Fortunately, there are bright spots that suggest a different attitude. A project in Costa Rica restored my optimism about a relevant role for the university and women of the university in new "feminine" or partnership priorities. Participation in the following projects supported by the University of Costa Rica suggested that things can be different: (1) a workshop jointly sponsored by the Presidential House, the University of Costa Rica, and the Carl Rogers Institute for Peace, which was seeking to facilitate dialogue between varying factions in the Central American conflicts; (2) a joint women-in-education seminar with a group from Norway who are advisors on a proposed law for Costa Rica Parliament consideration that includes a provision stating that since 50 percent of the population are women, 50 percent of the government seats should be filled by women; (3) a series of projects with women in the town of Gulfito who are seeking to improve their lot after the pullout of the major industry and the majority of the able-bodied men.

All of these projects were envisioned and undertaken by women within the university system. The issues addressed ranged from political and global to economic and local. The level of intense involvement and commitment was impressive. The larger impacts of all policies were considered. The voices of all concerned were included.

This was occurring in a country where many things are not convenient or available when it comes to following through on plans. The roads and the economy had not recovered from the hurricane of 1988. The university politics with male counterparts are still difficult. All of the women had child obligations. But none of them doubted the importance of their work or the university's role in getting involved on all these levels and in all of these projects at a personal, committed level.

There are examples of schools or programs within U.S. universities that are pursuing involved learning projects and responsible, partnership programs. More exist in women's universities, in particular, and in institutions with religious affiliations or women in development programs. But when we look at the whole picture, this kind of education remains the undernourished alternative to conventional patriarchal prioritized education.

Among institutions locked into intellectual fragmentation and behind parochial barriers there is a sense that something precious is missing. Some of the words of current "leading" university presidents suggest there are feelings that the tower may be locked up too tightly, or that (at least inside the castles) the fragmentation has gone too far. Eamon Kelly, President of Tulane University: "People are increasingly looking for a sense of community and shared purpose;" James O. Freeman, President of Dartmouth: "As faculty become more and more professionalized with their disciplines, it becomes more difficult to maintain (a pleasant) sense of community" (Wilson 1990, p. A8).

A recent article (Brauer 1990, p. B2) shows the underlying patriarchal longing for a more meaningful connection to the world. It is entitled "More Scholars Should Venture Forth to Confront, Enlighten, or Change the World," suggesting that the wisdom that is considered so precious and relevant inside the tower should be taken outside into the "real world." That seems encouraging, but there is no mention of learning *from* that real world. Dualism remains. The reified patriarchal point of view implies that the real world is a fixed object for manipulation. Co-existence and mutual nurturance are not part of the challenge in this attempt to open the minds and doors of the ivory towers.

IMPLICATIONS FOR NOURISHING LEARNING FROM THE VILLAGE STREETS TO THE IVORY TOWERS

Educational values that help clear the paths and build the bridges to global and self-understanding are profoundly simple. They are not new, but they may seem foreign to our recent experience if we have accepted that we have no options or opportunities for empowerment. The patriarchal educational culture has not recognized interrelationships as a productive force. Too often this dominator model in charge of teaching values labels nurturing and love as a regressive process, something that will hold back bold new ventures in academia.

Fortunately, we now have two decades of an enriched world of academic literature and research about and by women. It has clarified the "feminine" perspective as an indispensable one through authentic voices, ones dealing with survival. These voices can be given added volume and power through our efforts.

Collecting stories continues to help us identify the values that restore our integrity. Like gatherers, quilters, and reformers who have gone before, we can learn and enrich our lives by listening to and caring about others. Then we must take the responsibility to change our institutions, so they act with integrity as we face global challenges.

Seeing

First, we must get institutions and their faculties to truly see, as well as think, globally. We need to allow the profound awareness that the planet as a whole is our home to be in the forefront of our consciousness and our academic vision. This home is a living organism of interdependent communities, and all of us have some responsibility for its future. Education must be crosscultural, interdisciplinary, and personal. The illusion of security and sovereignty needs to be and will be redefined by personal experiences around the globe. For some lucky few it has been above the globe.

Seeing that the world is home, knowing that connection on a very integral level, seems to be more common among women in most cultures. Women, therefore, have an obligation to create opportunities for male partners to feel or sense this global intimacy. Sometimes there is great fear that with involvement or intimacy with such a grand concept, we will be left impotent or overwhelmed by the world. I can only report that empowerment, not impotency, comes with involvement. Therefore, our institutions of higher education must be encouraged to think, study, and create globally.

Feeling

Second, we must accept that the search for meaning is a valid, ongoing human adventure, one to be affirmed by academia. This allows for feelings and intuitions to be affirmed by an individual. These are essential to give us the impetus to look into and feel deeply about life. This is the search that lets us remain students our entire lives. It takes us through the ages and around the world. It keeps us fully alive. It is an open-ended, inclusive, stimulating experience of life.

This is akin to a major paradigm shift that Betty Reardon (1987, p. 18) says education must make. Education must stop seeking some "end-state." Real life is complex, vulnerable, and constantly changing. A system that is always focused on a final solution, to be put together in a fragmented but definite step-by-step process, inevitably leads to unnecessary frustration and no real understanding of how things work. Higher education must identify itself as a process, not a goal.

The rigidity of arbitrary and static relations within the structure of the university and the practice of placing publishing over teaching as an indication that one belongs as a mentor to human beings in a university must be questioned. Robert Muller, former Secretary General of the United Nations and President of the University for Peace in Costa Rica, has devised a world curriculum that addresses this (1987, p. 16). He states clearly that those in education must have a priority of transcending the material, scientific, and intellectual achievements and reaching deliberately into moral and spiritual spheres so that the soul and heart will want to learn. This has often been more identified as one aspect of the "feminine" domain. Those who are in touch with it must lead the way.

Sharing

Third, we must communicate and validate the value of the individual and interrelationships. Rooted in the confidence that comes from accepting self and others is a great survival skill. Inherent in acceptance is the possibility for working together and working through differences. The trust that results in validation of others and ourselves also replaces pseudo-validation evidenced in material or egotistical obsessions and hierarchical relationships.

The reality is that we are each human. We can understand and connect profoundly. We are free to learn, but we must ask ourselves what we want to learn. Is it what will help stuff a pocketbook someday, or is it what will fill our souls with wonder or save our planet? It does often seem that what we need to know for survival already exists among us. We learn more of what that is by sharing—our minds, our hearts, our curiosity. Women have had more practice, perhaps, and it may be the most basic issue of all to the mission of creating responsible educational priorities to help with global issues. A profound and prescient study by France Morrow (1990) entitled *Unleashing Our Unknown Selves* considers which dimensions of our humanness both men and women must recognize, accept, and cultivate to create a humane world.

Caring

Fourth, higher education needs to validate these first three values through engaging in social action. As Marilyn Ferguson reminds us in what should be required reading for everyone in higher education, *The Aquarian Conspiracy*, "the person and society are yoked, like mind and body" (1980, p. 90). We cannot separate or give more importance to one over the other. Therefore, persons transformed by this awareness must engage in social actions that address all aspects of our existence. Transformational leaders in higher education must listen to and act with our extended global family.

Accepting responsibility for the past and future and for others is the basis for creating the new conditions necessary for educational institutions to begin to envision a viable global future. Given the nature of these values and women's history with them in one way or another, women can more readily become the transformational leaders in greater numbers in higher education. Women have already begun to build the roads from the ivory towers to the village streets and to use them.

Ultimately, it is not a matter of male or female, or color or ethnicity, that allows an individual to be a transformational leader in education. These leaders will come from those who have walked the village streets, who have held the newborn and the dying, those who have looked at earth without boundaries, those who act without prejudice or revenge, and those who can keep a commitment to life.

11

The Status of Women in Chinese Universities

Roberta L. Weil

The Constitution adopted in 1982 states explicitly that women in China have equal rights in all spheres of life, whether political, economic, cultural or social, and that their rights and interests will be protected by the state.

However, traditional attitudes of male chauvinism, which predominated in China for several thousand years, have yet to be entirely eliminated; they are manifested in the continued existence of discrimination against and maltreatment of women.

Beijing Review, March 10, 1986

PREFACE

This chapter was originally written as a result of research conducted in China in 1987. The China of 1987 was attempting to take its place as one of the world's leading nations. The events of and since June 1989 have caused the world to look differently at China, even though many of China's official policies remain the same. The reader is advised, then, to keep in mind that the comments do not necessarily refer to the China of the 1990s. In addition, when discussing China one must always keep in mind its past history, the vastness of the nation, both in physical size and population, and the ethos of the people. China is not a nation easily destined for Western-style democracy. It is a nation whose doors and political methodology can open and close at the will of its leadership. In times of stress, the Chinese leadership turn to their old, tried, and true methods of constraint and control. The goals of modern China have not been changed substantially by the 1989 student uprising; the ways to achieve those goals have, in all likelihood, been modified.

INTRODUCTION

The People's Republic of China is a complex nation with a rich and fascinating heritage replete with values and traditions predating most of the world's present-day nations. The China of today is not the China of forty years ago, of one hundred years ago, or of centuries past. In the past hundred years China has moved from feudalism to revolution to socialism, from autonomy to vanquished to autonomy, from an open door policy to isolation to different types of openness, from a burgeoning educational system to a damnation of intellectuals, from a peasant society to rapid modernization. China is the most populous nation in the world, and one of its most valuable resources is its people, both men and women. Men in China have been the dominant sex, but since the turn of the century, and especially since Liberation in 1949, the role of women has changed drastically and for the better. Prior to 1949, Chinese women were held back under the thumbs of men as inferiors, incompetents, and, often, in positions of or near servitude. China today has an official policy of equal rights for women and of equal pay for equal work. Women in China are said to "hold up half the sky."

The purpose of this chapter is to present the role of women in higher education in China today, including their progress toward holding up half the sky, their values, attitudes, and beliefs. In order to offer a clear perspective on women in the past, I will begin with a historical discussion about women in China particularly during the last century.

Research for this chapter was conducted during an eight-week visit in 1987 to the People's Republic of China. During this time I visited twelve cities, eleven universities, and interviewed thirty-four women representing twelve diverse universities.

Women in higher education, for the purpose of this discussion, are defined primarily as faculty and administrators. I did have the opportunity, however, to interview graduate and undergraduate women students. Discussion of their plans, hopes, and frustrations and their perceptions of the future will also be included.

CONTEMPORARY HISTORICAL BACKGROUND

The year 1949 is that of Chinese Liberation, of the birth of the present-day People's Republic of China. For many, modern China begins then for it marked the end of the struggle for a class-free society. A class-free society should also be a society rid of religious and gender prejudices. Religion became, to an extent, the Communist party; those that continued to practice a formal religion did so in silence. Only in recent years has the government permitted open religious practice. As for gender prejudices, they did not magically disappear with Liberation. The All China Democratic Women's Federation in 1949 (see Croll 1974, p. 4) wrote, "We must overcome the weakness we inherited from the old generations such as narrow-mindedness, frailty, triviality, sense of reliance on others, susceptibility to sentiment, vagueness in political conceptions and lack of principles." Dispelling old myths meant dispelling old traditions and beliefs that often centered around the feudal marriage system. Old Chinese sayings like "noodles are not rice and women are not human beings," "a wife married is like a pony bought; I'll ride her and whip her as I like" (Croll 1975, pp. 31–32) conjure up vivid descriptions of beliefs about women. In 1949, in spite of the advances made since the early 1900s, denying women political and economic rights, holding them in servitude, and stripping them of the right even to manage the daily domestic affairs of their households were common but beginning to die out as women participated more fully in the revolutionary activities.

As women gained more power with Liberation two points of view on the focus of the women's movement emerged. The first was that women's organizations should concentrate on women's problems and welfare. The other was that women's associations should work toward the good of the nation, toward the overthrow of the feudal landlord class that oppressed all working people. Those espousing the latter view felt that women needed to raise their political consciousness and to increase their participation in the revolutionary struggles of the nation. Women could contribute to the demise of the feudal attitudes, customs, and habits by educating society. The first item on the agenda, however, was to establish revolutionary political power and then raise the position of the country's entire working class, increasing production and improving the quality of life. Special laws and measures often including special labor protection and conditions for working women were passed. Women responded positively to the post-Liberation call for their participation. They eagerly worked alongside men in the socialist revolution and construction of a new nation. Physically they moved into the working class in fields for which they were previously considered unfit.

Women in the country accounted for 30 percent of the basic improvement of farmland. In the cities they stepped out of their homes into small factories or production groups, into sports and the military. Educated women wholeheartedly stepped into education, science, health, medicine, literature, and art. As women began to take an active part in the country, the movement toward women holding up half the sky blossomed.

The Marriage Law of 1950 gave women even more freedom:

The Marriage Law unequivocally provides that the arbitrary and compulsory feudal marriage system which is based on the idea of the superiority of man over woman and which ignores the interests of the children shall be abolished; that bigamy, concubinage, child betrothal, interference with the remarriage of widows and the extraction of money or gifts in connection with marriage shall be prohibited; that the free choice of partners, monogamy, equal rights for both sexes and protection of the lawful interests of women and children shall be put into effect, so that husbands and wives may live in harmony, participate to the fullest extent in productive labour and rear united democratic families. (Croll 1975, p. 32)

Lifting the yokes of centuries past, the land reform and marriage laws intended to give women more autonomy and more power. Governmental sanction did not automatically give women these rights. Women who were deeded land often turned it over to men; those that tried to or actually had their marriages annulled found themselves shunned by society and turned away by their birth families, experiences shared by remarried widows.

By 1955, women progressed from unskilled laborers to trained workers as village schools for adults, continuation schools, training classes, and technical schools opened to women. They moved into a position of greater economic strength while they developed their latent capabilities. They were competing more and more with men in the workplace.

The nation's first Five-Year Program was put into effect in 1956. Men were urged to push ahead with their employment and women were urged to closely link their household work with the work of constructing a socialist society through the Five Goods Movement. This movement was evidence that the economy, and perhaps the society, were not ready to provide or fully support employment outside of the home for women. Phyllis Andors (in Wolf 1985, p. 21) lists the Five Goods as "(1.) unite with the neighborhood families for mutual aid; (2.) do housework well; (3.) educate children well; (4.) encourage family production, study and work; (5.) study well themselves." These Five Goods, aimed at raising the level and dignity of housework, cause one to think that they were also aimed at keeping women in their place, which was in the home and under the thumbs of men. This attempt to keep women in the home did fail, as many women continued with their determination to become active participants in the nation's economy and they continued to work outside the home. In reality, then as now, most families were unable to afford the luxury of one breadwinner.

During this period, China was greatly influenced by the Soviets in its movement toward socialism through reforms and modernizations. Higher education curricula reform aimed at ridding China of its bourgeois ideology. Higher education was reorganizing away from what had been a European/U.S. model toward the Soviet system. For teachers this meant the establishment of the Group of Design and Direction of Teaching (GDDT), which became the basic organization of the universities. A GDDT was composed of the teachers of a course and the research students in that field. Their task was to direct the teaching and research of that course of study. GDDTs greatly limited academic freedom as they focused on a centralized plan and control of subdued and humiliated teachers and obedient students. Teachers were also expected to work seventy hours a week in order to meet the needs of collective teaching and were not permitted any control of their classes or autonomy. Many of the professors of today were either educated under or taught under the GDDT system.

GDDT included a "Unified Entrance Enrollment and Unified Allocation of Graduates" plan (Chung 1953). Under this plan students were admitted to colleges and universities according to the present and future construction needs of the nation. Students could request three preferences for majors and, under each of these, five preferences for schools. Students throughout the nation took a centralized, organized, and unified entrance examination. Once admitted, students found themselves assigned to majors according to the country's needs, which only sometimes were in concert with their preferences.

The expectation was that graduates accept any assignment in the workforce, regardless of how incongruent that assignment might be with their studies. The nation's needs prioritized work allocations and graduates accepted the jobs assigned to them. Another expectation was for the student to put the needs of the country above his/her personal desires or needs, and since the government controlled the nation's payrolls that was easily achieved.

The Cultural Revolution spanned the decade from 1967 to 1977. It was a period in which, as *Time* Magazine (June 8, 1987) has declared, "China went mad." In a nation isolated from nearly all outside influences, people were beaten, tortured, imprisoned, and killed without benefit of trial or the protection of any legal system; families were separated and torn apart by humiliation and suffering. It was a period of peasant uprising against the feudal landlord and bourgeois society. Unfortunately for the educated—and those in education, the intellectuals—it was a time of uprising against them.

For women, it was a time of subjugation of their needs to those of the nation. Women were to be citizens of the nation and as such were to assist their husbands, to raise the children, to cause the family to uphold the morale of the nation, and, especially, to bring their children up to provide for the improved welfare of the nation. This raised women to a level only slightly above that which was proffered in 1956. Y. Li summed it up by writing, "The ultimate purpose of an individual's activities is for the good of the family, the country and society" (1981, p. 21). This is the prevailing belief and attitude of China officially and unofficially today. It may be one explanation for the strong loyalty expressed by so many Chinese today.

The Cultural Revolution had a strong impact on higher education. During the first four to five years the universities were closed. Many faculty were sent to the countryside for "re-education," to work and live as peasants. Sometimes their children went with them, although their teenage children were often sent to work in factories. Sometimes their children were sent to live with older relatives in distant cities. While families were often separated the adults were usually still with others from their work unit—the university. The elementary and secondary schools remained open, but any teaching or learning that went on in them was strictly accidental. Teachers at all levels were considered the lowliest of society because they were without political education. Discipline went by the wayside in all schools as children treated teachers as their parents did: with disrespect, humiliation, and, often, physical suffering. Professors and administrators were now without rank and were to stay that way until approximately 1982. Learning was expected to be by self-study and was especially not to be through the memorization and rote learning methods that had been so prevalent. When the universities did open, it was not to the usual cohort. Peasants and soldiers were sent to the universities as rewards for good work and to further even more the classless society by raising their educational level. The teachers encountered a new cohort of university students who were at or near the illiteracy level. The peasants, in particular, had come from the countryside where their education was minimal, since the need for field work was greater than the need for intellectual ability. Instead of teaching university topics, the teachers found themselves teaching reading, mathematics, language, and other basic subjects. The treatment of women teachers was no better and no worse than it was for men during this period.

In the final years of the Cultural Revolution, factory workers and other laborers were allowed to take the college entrance examinations. Those that passed entered the colleges and universities. Many of those that passed were children of intellectuals, people whose formal schooling was interrupted by the Cultural Revolution, losing vital education during the middle school years, or who had been cut off from higher education just as they were about to matriculate.

THE PRESENT

China is a dynamic nation moving rapidly toward industrial and eco-nomic modernization. It is important to remember that when changes are announced or new ideas implemented in China, the vastness of the nation, coupled with a centralized bureaucratic governmental admin-istration, causes changes to take months, sometimes years, to carry out. The old traditions and methods die out very slowly, regardless of the political system in place at a given time. To say that China is slow to change may be an understatement. New reforms or suggestions for reform regarding higher education are frequently announced. Some of these changes are implemented immediately at some universities. Other universities, so used to acting rather than reacting, will wait until the word filters down through official channels, usually through the Party organization.

China is also a nation in which individualism is less important than the good of the nation. Oftentimes this means that people will not take risks, will not be innovative, will not move ahead on something until it is not only official but commonplace.

Equal Pay for Equal Work

China today is very proud of its policy of equal pay for equal work. As with so many other nations, one must look at the definition of equal pay and equal work to truly understand the degree of equality; this means looking at the question of equal opportunity, a topic rarely raised in the past. Newspaper articles written in the late 1980s were beginning to address the problems facing women university graduates as they enter the workforce. The All China Women's Federation recently attacked the practice of sex discrimination against women graduates by work units (*China Daily*, August 1, 1987). This problem has existed continuously since Liberation but it is only recently that public acknowledgment has occurred. Even in private many women do not bring the subject up; with some, any discussion took place only after cautious prodding. The reason for this seems to be that regardless of the official policy today and regardless of the openness of the government, many Chinese over age forty remain discreet when talking against the government or in discussing practices contradictory to the official statements. They have been through the difficulty of the Cultural Revolution and they seem to fear a reiteration of that period. Most of the people I spoke with felt that a Cultural Revolution could not occur again in the same form, but they do believe that some type of reprisals are possible if the official policies change.

Women in China today say that they do receive equal pay for equal work. Margery Wolf (1985) states that equal pay for equal work is not the case. Wolf also found that men in Beijing with a middle school education earn 22 percent more than women with the same education, and the men in Shaoxing with the same education earn 18 percent more than the women. While equal pay for equal work is an issue more with Westerners than with the Chinese, the primary issue with both now is equal opportunity, a consideration previously ignored by the Chinese. The experiences of women in higher education can be considered as typical of women throughout the nation even though the work performed is considerably different. The definition of equal work also comes into play as women are often slotted into "women's" or "light work." "Light work" is generally any work that women do, regardless of how difficult or backbreaking it is. Planting tea and rice are among the most arduous jobs in China and they usually are filled by women, therefore considered "light work." Turning the knobs to run machinery is usually done by men and is considered "heavy work."

In higher education women can be found teaching and conducting research in probably all disciplines, just as one can find women in every type of job or career field in China, ranging from jet pilot to ditch digger. In education, as in all other fields, the level and the numbers of women in certain areas are what need to be observed, as they are found at the lower ends of the career and pay ladder. Regardless of the discipline, the women interviewed were universal in their responses about the scarcity of full professors or top administrators who are women. Concentrations of women can be found teaching in some disciplines, which have become like "light work" for the female laborer. The "light disciplines" at the university are the social sciences, the humanities, and languages.

The factors that have created or influenced women's lack of equal opportunity as evidenced by their placement in the workforce are several. Withholding the full measure of education from girls has been practiced for some time and continues through today. The role that the old values, traditions, and beliefs play is an important factor. Women's willingness to subjugate their significance to that of the nation is another factor. The use of pregnancy and motherhood as a rationale for not hiring or promoting women is common. Women also have the problem of the "second shift," which faces women all over the world. The "second shift" is the work done outside of paid employment: shopping for groceries and other household needs, caring for the children and for aging parents, doing laundry, cleaning house, and performing various other household duties. Finally, one must consider the practice of assigning people to jobs, which is done by local party officials and often biased by the "back door," or *guanshi*, method.

EQUAL EDUCATION OPPORTUNITY

Suzanne Pepper's research (1984) shows that in spite of the claims for equality made during the Cultural Revolution, between 1976 and 1980 fewer women than men were taking the college entrance examinations, fewer women were achieving passing scores, and the number of women gaining admission to the universities she visited was declining. She found that women represented one-third of the students taking the entrance examinations and 24 percent of the total college population. With regard to the question of quotas for women students, the universities denied the existence of a formal policy but two universities did suggest that informal minimum quotas of no less than 15 to 20 percent did exist at their universities.

The rationale for lowered numbers of women applicants is broad. One argument is that girls have traditionally been educated after the boys, and that practice has continued in the countryside today. Another is that girls do not do as well as boys in senior middle school and, therefore, cannot do well on the college entrance examinations. This is sometimes supported by an argument of physical and intellectual inferiority in which girls are considered more active in their learning in the early years with boys catching up and girls stopping learning in middle school. This argument is associated with a belief that women's brains are smaller than men's and that the girls' brains stop developing in the middle school years.

"China's employers 'prefer male grads.' So, varsities [meaning universities] may have to enroll fewer women students" was the August 1, 1987 headline in *The Straits Times*, a Singapore newspaper. The article reported the difficulty that many Chinese women graduates are having being placed in jobs. Several of the statements are particularly damning:

"Certain education officials have said that if the supply of these female graduates continues to exceed the demand among employers, then universities will be forced to cut back on the numbers of women in their recruitment," Mrs. Zhang said.

The People's Daily reported that more than 100 female graduates from the prestigious Beijing University and more than 80 percent of those from the Department of Journalism at Beijing's elite People's University were rejected this year by their assigned employers and had to be placed a second time.

Both Western observers and the official Chinese press have attributed the surge in open discrimination against female graduates to a new policy which gives employers a greater say in choosing university graduates, who used to be assigned by the state.

A few years ago, Chinese employers were able only to say that they preferred male graduates, but they now have the power to demand them and arbitrarily reject female employees assigned to them unless they are "beautiful" or "strong," the party newspaper said.

Many employers have gone so far as to specifically ask for poor male students instead of the outstanding female graduates assigned to them.

BELIEFS, VALUES, AND TRADITIONS

The women in China that I had the good fortune to interview have overcome many of the old beliefs, traditions, and values that plague their sisters in other fields of work. Westernization, modernization, or a technical society cannot totally remove the centuries of tradition ingrained in the Chinese of today. Those educated before Liberation have the advantage of a Western-style education that allowed for study in foreign countries. Many of their teachers were Westerners who brought with them Western views and information that were not available through Chinese teachers at that time.

The Lost Generation

During my interviews I met very few teachers between the ages of thirty-two and forty. Chinese born between 1947 and 1955, those that are thirty-two to forty years of age today, are a part of a lost generation in China. Denied their secondary and higher education because of the Cultural Revolution, they became, at its end, only one segment of Chinese desirous of and pleading for an education. I met many people in this age range working in clerical positions, as skilled laborers, and as taxi drivers; their career progress was greatly impeded by the Cultural Revolution. Many of the lost generation are struggling to better themselves and to make up for lost time. They are teaching themselves English and attending night school at their own expense, whereas university students pay little or no fees. The problems they face are not insurmountable but tenacity and strong determination will be necessary to achieve their goals.

The lost generation are unable to attend the university because they are older than the age limits set for undergraduate and graduate study, twenty-five and thirty-five years of age, respectively. These limitations have been set because China's universities can, at present, educate only about 5 percent of its college-age cohort. The limitations are caused by lack of teachers, inadequate number of universities, and limited dormitory space at the existing universities. Until 1985 all students had to live on campus. In 1985 many universities began requiring students whose homes are within a five-kilometer radius of the campus to live at home, thus freeing 20 to 25 percent of the dorm space (Farner 1985). All of this means that a very elite group of students, of ages approximately eighteen to twenty-two, are benefiting from a university education today.

WOMEN IN HIGHER EDUCATION TODAY

Women in higher education in China today are somewhat satisfied with where they are and with their career positions, even though they rarely had a choice since they were assigned first their course of college study and then their faculty position. They say that they earn equal pay for equal work, but they also assert almost unanimously that equal opportunity does not exist and that they have been or are being held back because of their gender. They are poorly represented in the upper professorial ranks and in administrative positions. They work very hard at their jobs and go home to the second shift. They are hoping to reach full professorships by retirement in order to retire with higher pay. They are aware of and recognize the inequities and inequalities and hope that the younger women can overcome some of the roadblocks. They are concerned that some of the changes occurring in the nation will hold women back even more. They are wives, mothers, grandmothers, daughters, sisters, and, sometimes, widows. Their relationships with their husbands show none of the past traditions of subservience. A few women actually outrank their husbands and some have achieved a measure of equality with regard to household work, so one cannot say that the inequality is absolutely universal, but it is the prevalent custom. The stories of the women interviewed serve to illustrate the lives—past, present, and future—of Chinese women in higher education today.

It is appropriate to comment at this point about the significance of studying abroad for teachers. Many of the women interviewed had studied in the United States or another English-speaking nation. Such study is important for several reasons. It allows a person to study beyond that which is generally available to them in China. It often permits them to obtain a degree not available in China. It is assumed by the Chinese that they will learn something more or better than they can at home, and the prestige attached to overseas study is very high. As much as Chinese universities are opening and moving forward, they are still behind in technological and educational advances. Unmentioned throughout any discussion with a Chinese about study abroad is the question of their returning to China. Nonreturning students are a growing problem and concern, both for the Chinese and for the host countries. That, however, is a topic outside of the realm of this chapter.

Included now is information about one of the young women students interviewed. Her plans and hopes for the future are presented along with her understanding of the reality of life for a young woman in China. Sun Yin, age twenty, is a senior in economics management at Hunan University, an interior key university. Her class of twenty is three-fourths male and she is the top student in the class. Her ambition is to get a position in the export business, which would seem very logical given her command of English, her intellect, and her other natural abilities.

The reality of her future is often stated by her male classmates, who taunt her with statements such as, "Why do you study so hard, you'll only end up teaching?" "You're going to get married and have a child so why do you make it hard on us to do better?" "You should give us a chance to be the best." She told me that regardless of her first job placement she is going to keep trying to get into the export field and will not give up her ambitions. In recent letters she expressed some of her thoughts:

All over the world, sex discrimination is more or less serious, even in China. Many of the female graduates were refused by the companies, factories—every level of working units, even by the association of women. The society regards them as the second class citizens. They are referred to as being dependent more on intuition and instinct to arrive at the decision than cool reasoning, unreliable and irrational. Nonsense of course. All of this really frustrated some of the aggressive women. In fact, women have succeeded in almost any kind of job you care to name, which really put the biased men to shame. God grants every one equal status, and we should cherish it. No matter what will happen, our women should fight hard against prejudice. (August 31, 1987)

I hope to be a career woman, a wife and a mother for years to come. But your idealism has to be adapted to the present society. In many respects, what you want to reach is restricted by many factors such as the traditional habits and forms, moral standards (in case of your showing up in public so frequently), the current background, etc.—even though I don't like to be mediocre and unambitious and seem to be a bit out of class. While in some ways I am not as competent as men, I prefer to try through my efforts no matter what the results might be. There is a will, there is a hope.

Our party Congress just ended hastening the process of the political reform. Our party intended to free itself from day-to-day administration affairs and decentralize its power to the locality. I assumed from your trip of China you can feel how bureaucracy and red-tape and "backdoor" blocked down the process of development of our country. I just stand at a crucial point at present waiting for the assignment by our government.

My future is not up to me. Probably my fate will be resigned by someone somewhere. It is rather a complicated procedure you can't imagine, during which "backdoor" relationship really plays a large role. If your parents or relatives know the key person in the Engineering Committee running our university, they will "advertise" you hoping to get a position in Committee (or company factories under it.) Then the cadres both in our university and in our department have the power to decide where you will be. It lies in your connection with them. As you always follow their instructions and are never against them, you might be a bit more lucky than those who neither have some background in the Committee nor get along well with the cadres. Your fate is at their discretion. Under this circumstance, you are so tired to be disturbed by this kind of ugly thing and also it will give rise to low efficiency of our work. Have you found that your credits and your devotion in the past four years proof [sic] nothing?

On the other hand, I am a bit self-made, avoiding involvement in the political affairs and being influenced by the inherent surroundings. As a matter of fact, I show my concern to them to get rid of the effects of the countless changes, the ups and downs of one group today instead of another yesterday. I believe at least I can devote something to our society, to our human beings through the individual development, the realization of personal value. I should absorb more and more books and broaden my mind and enrich my experience and so on to perfect myself. There is a far long way to go, but I should be confident. (November 2, 1987)

CONCLUSION

"Most employers are loathe to hire women because they are likely to marry and have children, events which are still seen as a liability and a financial burden for the work unit" (*The Straits Times*, August 1, 1987). This quote is indicative and illustrative of the problems young university women in China face today. It also conveys the message that China has not advanced too far in treating its women as equals to men. The subtle methods of discrimination that the women interviewed have experienced and that their lives illustrate are becoming more overt. This is causing women and the nation to become more conscious of such activities. To date, however, no positive means of combating the discrimination has been brought forth. Instead, some of the means of opening up the employment field with freer choice of employment seem to be aiding discriminatory action.

Women in higher education have, in many ways, had the advantage over their counterparts in other fields. They have had the benefits of an education, they have worked in pleasant surroundings, and even those who did not choose education have adjusted to their careers and found them satisfying, challenging, and rewarding. They have earned equal pay for equal work. Like their counterparts in other careers, they have not had equal opportunity. The most desirable university positions go overwhelmingly to their male colleagues, regardless of their experience, ability, education, age, or length of service. Preferential treatment is accorded men because they are men.

Since 1900 China has experienced considerable progress in all aspects of society, and the issue of equality is certainly far less serious than previously. Women have not progressed as much as the nation nor as much as men, but they have progressed. There are strong disparities between the official policy of equal opportunity and the informal practice of inequality and inequities that women continue to face. The influence of the old values and traditions is strong. Women in higher education in China today do hold up half the sky and more. They provide service to their nation through their personal and their professional lives. They do the same work as men and go home to the second shift, which takes time and energy away from them. But they are not given the responsibility, the recognition, or the remuneration that comes with their full-time positions, their fulfillment of the second shift, and their role in moving China forward, their contribution to China's society. In spite of this, they continue to achieve and to contribute to society. As contact with Westerners increases and as more of society shares in the bounty of modernization, the women are likely to feel less satisfied with their positions. The women interviewed give evidence of a small but growing restlessness and unhappiness with the status quo and also give evidence of what China can achieve if women are granted full equality and opportunity.

Universities Visited

Beijing Foreign Studies University, Beijing
Beijing Normal University, Beijing
Changchun College of Geology, Jilin
Chengdu Institute of Physical Culture, Chengdu
Huazhong University of Science and Technology, Wuhan
Hunan University, Nanjing
Northeastern Forestry University, Harbin
Northwestern University, Xi'an
Shanghai International Studies University, Shanghai
Wuhan University, Wuhan
Zhongshan University, Guangzhou

Bibliography

Aguirre, A., Jr. (1987). "An interpretative analysis of Chicano faculty in academe." *The Social Science Journal* 24, no. 1, 71–81.

Almquist, E. M. (1984). "Further consequences of double jeopardy: The reluctant participation of racial-ethnic women in feminist organizations." In A. W. Van Horne (ed.), *Ethnicity and Women*, pp. 113–34.

Amaro, H., and Russo, N. F. (1987). "Hispanic women and mental health." *Psychology of Women Quarterly* 11, 393–407.

Amaro, H., Russo, N. F., and Pares-Avila, J. (1987). "Contemporary research on Hispanic women: A selected bibliography of the social science literature." *Psychology of Women Quarterly* 11, 523–32.

American Council on Education. (1987). *Annual Study of American Colleges and Universities.* Washington, DC: ACE. Unpublished Report.

Anderson, M. (1985). "New York Times," July 22, 1951. In Bernard E. Farber (ed.), *A Teacher's Treasury of Quotations.* Jefferson, NC and London: McFarland and Company, Inc.

Antonucci, T. (1980). "The need for female models in education." In Sari Knopp Biklen and Marilyn B. Brannigan (eds.), *Women and Educational Leadership* pp. 185–95. Lexington, MA: D. C. Heath.

Aptheker, B. (1982). *Woman's Legacy.* Amherst: University of Massachusetts Press.

Aptheker, H. (ed.). (1973). *A Documentary History of the Negro People in the United States,* vol. 1. New York: The Citadel Press.

Austin, H. S., and Bayer, A. E. (1972). "Sex discrimination in academe." *Educational Record* 53, no. 2, 101–18.

Ayscough, F. (1937). *Chinese Women Yesterday and Today*. Boston: Houghton Mifflin Co.

Bam, E. E. (1982). *Basotho Primary School Children and their Conservation of Mass, Weight, Liquid and Number*. Unpublished master's thesis, National University of Lesotho.

Bandura, A., and Walters, R. (1963). *Social Learning and Personality Development*. New York: Holt, Rinehart & Winston.

Bass, B. M. (1985). *Leadership and Performance beyond Expectations*. New York: Free Press.

Bass, B. M., and Avolio, B. J. (1985). *The Multifactor Leadership Questionnaire*. Palo Alto, CA: Consulting Psychologists Press.

Benezet, L. T., Katz J., and Mangusson, F. W. (1981). *Style and Substance—Leadership and the College Presidency*. Washington, DC: American Council on Education.

Bennis, W., and Nanus, B. (1985). *Leaders: The Strategies of Taking Charge*. New York: Harper and Row.

Berry, M. F., and Blassingame, J. W. (1982). *Long Memory: The Black Experience*. New York: Oxford University Press.

Bliss, B., and Docherty, E. M. (1979). "Conservation of mass, weight, and volume in Yoruba adolescents." *Child Study Journal* 9, no. 2, 85–91.

Bodley, J. (1982). *Victims of Progress*. Palo Alto, CA: Mayfield Publishing.

Bogart, K. (1989). "Toward equity in academe: An overview of strategies for action." In Carol Pearson, Donna Shavlik, and Judith Toucton (eds.), *Educating the Majority*, pp. 384–99. New York: American Council on Education and Macmillan Publishing Co.

Brauer, C. (1990). "More scholars should venture forth to confront, enlighten, or change the world." *The Chronicle of Higher Education*. March 14. Vol. XXXVI.

Bronstein, P., Black, L., Pfennig, J., and White, A. (1986). "Getting academic jobs: Are women equally qualified—and equally successful?" *American Psychologist* 41, no. 3, 318–22.

Broyelle, C. (1977). *Women's Liberation in China*. Preface by Han Suyin. Translated from the French by Michele Cohen and Gary Herman. Atlantic Highlands, NJ: Humanities Press.

Brubaker, J. S., and Rudy, W. (1976). *Higher Education in Transition*. New York: Harper and Row.

Budge, E. A. W. (1967). *The Egyptian Book of the Dead*. New York: Dover Publications, Inc.

Bureau of the Census. (1989). Washington, DC Office of Bureau of Census.

Burns, J. M. (1985). *Leadership*. New York: Harper and Row.

Carter, B., Insko, K., Loeb, D., and Tobias, M. (Eds). (1989). *A Dream Compels Us: Voices of Salvadoran Women*. San Francisco. CA: New America Press.

Castaneda, C. (1972). *Journey to Ixtlan: The Lessons of Don Juan*. New York: Simon and Schuster.

Center for Education Statistics. (April 1988). *Survey Report*. Washington, DC: U.S. Department of Education, Office of Educational Research and Improvement.

Chamberlain, M. (ed.). (1988). *Women in Academe: Progress and Prospects*. New York: Russell Sage Foundation.

Chase, P. (1987). *Black Women College Presidents: Perceptions of Their Major Job Roles, Problems, Expectations and Experiences*. Unpublished doctoral dissertation, Harvard University, Boston.

Chase-Riboud, B. (1979). *Sally Hemings*. New York: A Seaver Book/The Viking Press.

Chi, P. (1977). *Chinese Women in the Fight for Socialism*. Peking: Foreign Languages Press.

Chu, L. (1985). *Rural Women's Vocational Training for National Development*. University Park: New Mexico State University.

Chung, S. (1953). *Higher Education in Communist China*. Kowloon, Hong Kong: Union Research Institute.

Churchward, A. (1978). *The Signs and Symbols of Primordial Man*. Westport, CT: Greenwood Press Inc.

Cole, R. V., Jr. (April 1, 1984). "A Comparison of Perceived Leadership Styles among Presidents of Selected Black Colleges in the Southwestern and Southeastern United States." Paper presented at the Annual Meeting of the American Educational Research Association, New Orleans, LA. ERIC ED 244 532.

Conference Report. *Signs*, Autumn 1988.

Croll, E. (1975). *The Women's Movement in China: A Selection of Readings, 1949–1973*. Nottingham, England: Anglo-Chinese Educational Institute, Modern China Series No. 6, Russell Press Ltd.

Daniel, S. I. (1970) *Women Builders*. Washington, DC: The Associated Publishers

Diop, C. A. (1959). *The Cutural Unity of Black Africa*. Chicago: Third World Press.

Downton, J. V. (1973). *Rebel Leadership: Commitment and Charisma in a Revolutionary Process*. New York: Free Press.

DuBois, W. E. B. (1903). "The talented tenth." In *The Negro Problem*. New York: James Pott and Company.

Eisler, R. (1988). *The Chalice and the Blade: Our History, Our Future*. San Francisco, CA: Harper and Row.

Escobedo, T. H. (1980). "Are Hispanic women in higher education the nonexistent minority?" *Educational Researcher*, no. 9, 7–12.

Espin, O. M. (1987). "Psychological impact of migration on Latinas." *Psychology of Women Quarterly* 11, 489–503.

Estrada, L. (1988). "Anticipating the demographic future: dramatic changes are on the way." *Change* May/June, p. 14–19.

Estrada, L.F. (1984). "The extent of Spanish/English bilingualism in the United States." *Aztlan* 15, no. 2, 379–391.

Fahrmeier, E. D. (1978). "The development of concrete operations among the Hausa." *The Journal of Cross-Cultural Psychology* 9, no. 2, 23–44.

Ferguson, M. (1980). *The Aquarian Conspiracy: Personal and Social Transformation in Our Time*. Los Angeles, CA: J.P. Tarcher, Inc.

Fernandez, John P. (1981). *Racism and Sexism in Corporate Life: Changing Values in American Business*. Lexington, MA: Lexington Books.

Fields, C. (1988). "This Hispanic pipeline—narrow, leaking and needing repair." *Change*, May/June, p 20–27.

Fisher, J. L. (1988), *Power of the Presidency*. NY: MacMillan.

Fobbs, J. M. J. (1988). *The Top-Line Women Administrators in Public and Private Two-Year Institutions of Higher Education: Their Perceptions of the Managerial Style and Leadership Skill that Contributed to Executive Appointment*. Unpublished doctoral dissertation, Ohio State University, Columbus.

Giddings, P. (1984). *When and Where I Enter: The Impact of Black Women on Race and Sex in America*. New York: William Morrow.

Gilligan, C. (1982). *In a Different Voice*. Cambridge, MA: Harvard University Press.

Gilligan, C., and Attanucci, J. (1988). "Two moral orientations: Gender differences and similarities." *Merrill-Palmer Quarterly* 34, 223–37.

Green, B. M. (1969). "Upgrading Black women in the supervisory ranks." *Personnel*, November-December, 47–50.

Gross, S., and Bingham, M. (1980). *Women in Traditional China*. Hudson, WI: Gary E. McCuen, Publisher.

Half the Sky. (1985). Beijing: Women of China.

Hamilton, R. S. (1987). Challenges and Opportunities: A Profile of Women in the World. Selected proceedings and position papers from International Women's Conference "Women to Women: Simple Parenting from a Global Perspective." Delta Research & Educational Foundation. Delta Sigma Theta Society, Inc. Washington, DC.

Hater, J. J., and Bass, B. M. (1988). "Superior's evaluations and subordinates' perceptions of transformational and transactional leadership." *Journal of Applied Psychology* 73, no. 4, 695–702.

Hayes-Bautista, D. (1980). "Identifying 'Hispanic' populations: The influence of research methodology upon public policy." *American Journal of Public Health* 70, 353–56.

Hayslip, L. L. with Wurts, C. J. (1989). *When Heaven and Earth Changed Places: A Vietnamese Woman's Journey from War to Peace*. New York: Penguin.

Heller, T. (1982). *Women and Men as Leaders*. South Hadley, MA: J. F. Bergin.

Henderson, H. (1988). "Thinking globally, acting locally: The politics and ethics of the solar age." *Women of Power*. 11, 34–45.

Hennig, M., and Jardin, A. (1976). *The Managerial Woman*. New York: Anchor.

Heron, A., and Simonsson, M. (1969). "Weight conservation in Zambian children: A nonverbal approach." *International Journal of Psychology* 4, no. 4, 282–92.

Hetherington, C., and Barcelo, R. (1985). "Womentoring: A cross-cultural perspective." *Journal of the National Association of Women Deans and Counselors* 49, no. 1, 12–15.

History. (1982). Compiled by the China Handbook Editorial Committee. Translated by Dun J. Li. Beijing: Foreign Languages Press.

Howe, F. (1984). *Myths of Coeducation: Selected Essays 1964–1983*. Bloomington: Indiana University Press.

Illich, I. (1982). *Gender*. New York: Pantheon.

Jackson, J.G. (1970). *Introduction to African Civilization*. Secaucus, NJ: The Citadel Press.

Janeway, E. (1986). "Prioritizing the world." *Chronicle of Higher Education*, 12/17, p 42.

John, M., Dambe, M., Polhemus, S., and John, F. (1983). "Children's thinking in Botswana." *Bolewsa Educational Research Journal*, 2, no. 1 p.3–17.

Johnson, C. (1989). "Consider all your options." Paper presented at the Second Annual Meeting of the International Conference on Women in Higher Education, San Diego, California.

Jones, M. C. (1991). *An Exploratory and Descriptive Study of the Cognitive Attributes, Life Experiences, and Leadership Styles of Black Women College Presidents.* Unpublished doctoral dissertation, George Washington University, Washington, DC.

Josefowitz, N. (1980). *Paths to Power.* Reading, MA: Addison-Wesley.

Kagan, J. (1987). "Taking charge of change: How the new role definitions for women are created by women." *Working Woman* 12, 53–54.

Kanter, R. M. (1977). *Men and Women of the Corporation.* New York: Basic Books.

Keefe, S. E., and Padilla, A. M. (1987). *Chicano Ethnicity.* Albuquerque: University of New Mexico Press.

Kheel, M. (1988). "From healing herbs to deadly drugs." *Women of Power*, 11, 34–45.

Kingston, M. H. (1977). *The Woman Warrior: Memoirs of a Girlhood among Ghosts.* New York: Alfred A Knopf.

Leakey, R., and Levin, R. (1978). *People of the Lake: Mankind and Its Beginnings.* New York: Doubleday.

Lee, V. (1985). "Access to higher education: The experience of blacks, Hispanics and low socio-economic status whites." Washington, DC: American Council on Education, Division of Policy Analysis and Research.

Lerner, G. (1973) *Black Women in White America.* New York: Random.

Lerner, G. (1977). *The Female Experience: An American Documentary.* Indianapolis: Bobbs-Merrill.

Li, Y. (1981). *Historical Roots of Changes in Women's Status in Modern China.* Jamaica, NY: Center of Asian Studies, St. John's University.

Loden, M. (1985). *Feminine Leadership, or How to Succeed in Business without Being One of the Boys.* New York: Random House.

Loewenberg, B. J., and Bogin, R. (eds.). (1976). *Black Women in Nineteenth Century Life: Their Words, Their Thoughts, Their Feelings.* University Park: Pennsylvania State University Press.

Maduro, M. (1988). "Women, technology, and the global economy." *Women of Power*, 11, p 53–55.

Malizio, A. G. (1988). "Facts in brief: One quarter of all employed scientists are women." *Higher Education and National Affairs* 37, no. 7, 3.

Martin, J. (1982). "Excluding women from the educational realm." *Harvard Educational Review.* Vol. 52, No. 2, p. 133–42.

McGee, M. (1979). *The Woman College President in 1978: Her Personal Characteristics, Her Professional Characteristics, Her Career Pattern and Opinion of Her Role.* Unpublished doctoral dissertation, University of Florida, Gainesville.

McKissick, F. (1969). *Three-fifths of a Man.* Toronto: McMillian.

McMillen, L. (1987). "Universities are lagging in hiring women and blacks for faculty jobs." *Chronicle of Higher Education*, 7/8, p 11–12.

Miche, M. (1988). "Look before you leap: Graduates pledge to think responsibly about career decisions." *Breakthrough*, Vol. 10, 1, p 85.

Mies, M. (1986). *Patriarchy and Accumulation on a World Scale*. London: ZedBooks.

Miller, J. B. (1976). *Toward a New Psychology of Women*: Boston: Beacon Press.

Mischel, W. (1970). "Sex-typing and socialization." in P. H. Mussen (ed.), *Carmichael's Manual of Child Psychology*, 3d ed., vol. 2, pp. 3–60. New York: John Wiley and Sons.

Monroe, S., and Goldman, P. (1988). *Brothers*. New York: William Morrow and Co.

Moore, J. (1990). "Hispanic/Latino: Imposed label or real identity?" *Latino Studies Journal* 1, no. 2, 33–47.

Morrow, F. (1991). *Unleashing our Unknown Selves: An Inquiry into the Future of Femininity and Masculinity*. New York: Praeger Press.

Moses, Yolanda T. (1989). "Black women in academe: Issues and strategies." In *Association of American Colleges, Project on the Status and Education of Women*. New York: Ford Foundation.

Muller, R. (1987). "Excerpts from a world core curriculum." *Breakthrough*. A publication of global education associates. New York, 8, 3–4.

Mundschenk, D. (1978). *Creative Journaling, an Exploration of Personal Consciousness Through Perception and Integrity*. Ann Arbor, Michigan: University Dissertation Microfilms.

Myers, I. B., and Briggs, K. (1977). *The Myers-Briggs Type Indicator*. Palo Alto, CA: Consulting Psychologists Press.

Napier, S. R. (1979). *Perceived Leadership Effectiveness among Selected Predominantly Black Women Administrators and Institutional Variables in Higher Education: An Exploratory Study*. Unpublished doctoral dissertation, University of Tennessee, Knoxville.

New Women in China. (1972). Peking: Foreign Languages Press.

Nsibandze, E. N., and John, M. (1985). "Cultural influences on children's thinking in Swaziland." *Boleswa Educational Research Journal* 5, 36.

Office of Women in Higher Education. (1988). *Women Chief Executive Officers in U.S. Colleges and Universities*. Washington, DC: American Council on Education.

Olivas, M. A. (1988). "Latino faculty at the border." *Change*, May/June p 29–33.

Ortiz, F. I. (1983). "Restraining and liberating perceptions regarding minority women's institutional participation." Paper presented at the Annual Meeting of the American Educational Research Association, Montreal, Canada.

———. (1988). "Hispanic American women in higher education: A consideration of the socialization process." *Aztlan* 17, no. 2, 125–52.

Otaala, B. (1973). "The development of operational thinking in primary school children." In *An Examination of Some Aspects of Piaget's Theory among the Iteso Children of Uganda*. New York: Teachers College Press.

Overholt, C., Anderson, M., Cloud, K., and Austin, J. (eds.) (1985). *Gender Roles in Development Projects: A Case Book*. West Hartford, CT: Kumarian Press.

Padilla, F. (1985). *Latino Ethnic Consciousness*. Notre Dame, IN: Notre Dame Press.

Pearson, C., Shavlik, D., and Touchton, J. (1989). *Educating the Majority*. New York: American Council on Education and Macmillan Publishing Co.

Peck, S. (1985). *Halls of Jade, Walls of Stone, Women in China Today*. New York: Franklin Watts.

Pepper, Suzanne. (1984). *China's Universities: Post-Mao Enrollment Policies and Their Impact on the Structure of Secondary Education*. Ann Arbor: Center for Chinese Studies, University of Michigan.

Phagan, P. A. (1982). "Profile of the female president in higher education." *Dissertation Abstracts, International*. University Microfilms #82–09400.

Ploski, H. A., and Warren, M., II (eds.). (1976). *The Negro Almanac: A Reference Work on the Afro-American*. New York: Bellwether.

Quezada, R., Loheyde, K. J., and Kacmaczyk M, (1984). "The Hispanic woman graduate student: Barriers to mentoring in higher education." *Texas Tech of Education* 11, no. 3, 235–41.

Ralston, Y. L. (1974). *An Analysis of Attitudes as Barriers to the Selection of Women as College Presidents in Florida*. Unpublished doctoral dissertation, University of South Florida, Tampa.

Reardon, B. (1987). "Excellence in education through peace making." *Breakthrough*. A publication of global education associates, New York: 8, 3–4.

Rosa, P. E., and Smith, E. E. (1989). "Equity and pluralism: Full participation of blacks and Hispanics in New England higher education." In *Task Force Report of the New England Board of Higher Education*.

Rose, S. M. (1985). "Professional networks of junior faculty in psychology." *Psychology of Women Quarterly* 9, 533–47.

Rossi, A. (1987). "Coeducation in a gender-stratified society." In lasser (ed.), *Educating Men and Women Together: Coeducation in a Changing World*, pp. 11–34. Urbana and Chicago: University of Illinois Press.

Ruble, T. L., Cohen, R., and Ruble, D. N. (1984). "Sex stereotypes: Occupational barriers for women." *American Behavioral Scientist* 27, no. 3, 339–56.

Sagaria, Mary Ann D. (1988). "Administrative mobility and gender." *Journal of Higher Education* 59, no. 3, 340–411.

Salinger, J. D. (1951). *Catcher in the Rye*. Boston: Little Brown.

Sandler, B., and Hall, R. (1982). *The Classroom Climate: A Chilly One for Women?* Washington, DC: Project on the Status and Education of Women, Association of American Colleges.

———. (1984). *Out of the Classroom: A Chilly Campus Climate for Women?* Washington, DC: Project on the Status and Education of Women, Association of American Colleges.

———. (1986). *The Campus Climate Revisited: Chilly for Women Faculty, Administrators, and Graduate Students*. Washington, DC: Project on the Status and Education of Women, Association of American Colleges.

Sargent, A. G. (1981). *The Androgynous Manager*. New York: AMACOM.: A Division of the American Management Association.

Schaef, A. W. (1985). *Women's Reality: An Emerging Female System in a White Male Society*. Minneapolis, MN: Wilson Press.

Seeds of Promise: The Critical Roles of Third World Women in Food Production. (1988). Videotape and discussion guide. Washington, DC: OEF International.

Shina, V. (1988). "A biological link." *Women of Power* 11, 19–21.

Simeone, A. (1986). *Academic Women Working toward Equality*. Westport, CT: Bergin & Garvey.

Simoniella, K. (1981). "On investigating the attitudes toward achievement and success in eight professional U.S. Mexican women." *Aztlan* 12, no. 1, 121–37.

Smedley, A. (1976). *Portraits of Chinese Women in Revolution*. Edited with an introduction by Jan MacKinnon and Steve MacKinnon. Afterword by Florence Howe. Old Westbury, N.Y.: The Feminist Press.

Snapp, S. (1988). "The feminization of farming in Nicaragua." *Women in Power*, 11, 37–41.

Spivac, G. (1987). *Other Worlds: Essays in Cultural Politics*: New York: Routledge.

Stanford News. (March 2, 1988). Stanford University News Service.

Swoboda, M. J., and Milar, S. B. (1986). "Networking-mentoring: Career strategy of women in academic administration." *Journal of NAWDAC*, 50(1) 8–13.

Swuderski, W. (1988). "Problems faced by women in gaining access to administrative positions in education." *Education Canada*, Fall/Autumn, 25–31.

Taban, L. (1982). "Africa: Fastest in growth rate." *Populi* 9, no. 1, 3–26.

Tessler, S. E. (1976). *Profiles of Selected Women College Presidents Reflecting the Emerging Role of Women in Higher Education*. Unpublished doctoral dissertation, Boston College, Boston.

The World's Women. 1970–1990. (1991.) NY: United Nations Publication.

Tierney, W. G. (1988). "Organizational culture in higher education." *Journal of Higher Education* 59, no. 1, p. 2–21.

Tinker, I. (1988). *Feminizing Development—For Growth with Equity. Care Briefs on Development Issues*, vol. 6. New York: Care Headquarters.

Udokang, P. (ed.). (1985). *Women in Industry: North-South Connections. A Study by the North-South Institute*. Ottawa, Canada: North-South Institute.

Ulich, R. (1941). "Some thoughts on education for girls." *Harvard Educational Review* 11, no. 3, p 273–77.

United States Department of Commerce, Bureau of the Census. (1989). *The Hispanic Population in the United States*. Current Population Reports, Series P–20. No. 444.

Valverde, L. (1988). "The missing element; Hispanics at the top in higher education." *Change*, May/June, p. 11.

Walker, M. (1966). *Jubilee*. Boston: Houghton Mifflin.

Washington, B. T. (1901). *Up from Slavery*. New York: A. L. Burt.

Welch, M. S. (1980). *Networking*. Harcourt & Brace Jovanovich.

Westervelt, E. (1974). "The higher education of women: Carnegie study." *Harvard Educational Review* 44, no. 2, 294–313.

Wilkerson, M. B. (1984). "Lifting as we climb: Networks for minority women." In A. Tinsley, C. Secor, and S. Kaplan (eds.), *Women in Higher Administration*. No. 45, March, pp. 59–66.

Willie, C. V., and Edmonds, R. R. (eds.). (1978). *Black Colleges in America*. New York: Teachers College, Columbia University.

Wilson, R. (1990). "Quality of life said to have diminished on U.S. campuses." *The Chronicle of Higher Education*. May 2, XXXVI, no. 3.

Wolf, Margery. (1985). *Revolution Postpones Women in Contemporary China*. Stanford, CA: Stanford University Press.

Wolf, Margery, and Witke, Roxane. (1975). *Women in Chinese Society*. Stanford, CA: Stanford University Press.

Woods, S. (1982). *Career Patterns and Attitudes of Women Who Are College Presidents*. Unpublished doctoral dissertation, Rutgers University, New Brunswick, New Jersey.

Zikmund, Barbara B. (1988), "The well-being of academic women is still being sabotaged by colleagues, by students and by themselves." *The Chronicle of Higher Education*, September 1, p. A–44.

Index

abolitionists, 28, 122

acculturation, of Hispanics, 81

administration, university: and
Affirmative Action policies, 86–87;
African American women, 25, 28–
39, 61–67; chain of command, 20–
21; Chinese women, 138, 141;
composition, 6, 13, 15, 56, 61–63;
Hispanas, 72, 79, 92; upward
mobility, 17–19, 43; White Male
System, 13–22

Affirmative Action policies (AAP/
EEO), 17–20, 76, 79, 86–87, 93,
103

Africa, 26–27, 107–8, 110–13, 119

African American women: aesthetic,
54–56; authority in the classroom,
49–52; campus climate and support
groups, 9–11; college presidents,
61–67; communication challenges,
41–59; early educational leaders,
28–38; faculty, 42, 49–52, 79–80;

history of, 26–38; schools and
colleges, 28–36; slavery, 27–28;
stereotypes, 14–17, 50, 52, 65;
students, 52–56; university
administrators, 25–26, 28–39,
61–67; and the White Male
System, 15–16

agriculture. *See* food production and
distribution

All China Women's Federation, 137

Anderson, Marian, 42

The Androgynous Manager (Sargent),
66

Angelou, Maya, 58–59

Asians, percent in United States
university faculty, 79–80

assimilation, of Hispanics, 81

Association of American Colleges
(AAC), 5

atmosphere, campus. *See* climate,
campus

autonomy, and femininity, 88

About the Editor and Contributors

Lynne Brodie Welch is currently Dean, School of Nursing at Marshall University. Her prior positions include: Director of Nursing Programs for the South Carolina Area Health Education Consortium; Dean and Professor, College of Nursing and Allied Health at the University of Texas at El Paso; Dean, School of Nursing, Southern Connecticut State University; Chairperson and Associate Professor, Baccalaureate Nursing, Pace University, Pleasantville; and Assistant Professor of Nursing, Western Connecticut State University. She received her doctorate from Teachers College, Columbia University, her master's from Catholic University of America and her bachelor's degree from the University of Connecticut. She has served on a variety of professional and community boards and committees. She has published in a variety of journals, monographs, and symposia.

Dee Aker is Dean of Academic Affairs at the University of Humanistic Studies. Her interest is in the role for women in higher education with the world community of women. She has extensive experience with women in Third World nations.

Patricia Bassett is Assistant to the Vice President for Student Affairs at Southern Illinois University at Carbondale. Her involvement in issues in higher education for ethnic minority women is extensive. She has published on issues related to African American women in higher education.

Martha Tyler John is Dean of the School of Education and Human Services at Marymount University. Her research was conducted while she served as a Fulbright Professor in Botswana and later as Department Chairperson of Educational Foundations and Management at the University of Swaziland.

M. Colleen Jones is a doctoral student at George Washington University. She is an American College of Education National Improvement Program for Women fellow. Her research focuses on black women presidents of colleges and universities in the United States.

Anita Leal is Director of Employee Support Programs at the University of California, Santa Cruz. Previously she was an assistant professor at the University of Iowa in the Counselor Education Department. Her research interests center around the role of Hispanic women in higher education.

Barbara Matthews is a counselor at Southern Connecticut State University in the Counseling and Career Planning Department. She has served as a counselor, an advisor to the Black Student Union, and either a member or friend of Networking and Support groups for women of color.

Cecilia Menjivar is a doctoral student in Sociology at the University of California, Davis. Her areas of research are demography, development in international migration and social networks among immigrants.

Eleanor J. Smith is Vice President for Academic Affairs and Provost at William Paterson College. She has taught and lectured widely on topics related to the historical experience of African Americans and specifically African American women.

Paul M. Smith, Jr. is Professor of Afro-American Studies and Psychology at the University of Cincinnati.

Sarah Nieves-Squires is a professor in the Ferebe Scholars Program at Simmons College. Her area of interest is Hispanic women and their role in institutions of higher education.

Roberta L. Weil is an assistant to the dean of graduate studies and research at the University of California, San Diego, where she is responsible for graduate student admissions and academic affairs. Her current interests are higher education management, women in higher education, and a continuing interest in China.

Denise Wilbur is Director of Institutional Research at the College of St. Thomas. Her research focuses on the campus climate for women and minorities.

Mary Ann Williams is an associate professor of communications in the Black Studies Department of the Ohio State University. Her research interests are communication patterns between and within ethnic groups in the United States.